Praise for *Making Every Primary Lesson Count*

I really like two specific things about this book. The first thing is that at its heart is a list of six important principles: challenge, explanation, modelling, practice, feedback and questioning. The discussions around these educational touchstones create a very useful guide which transcends top tips and quick fixes – inviting the reader to think for themselves. The second thing is that it is written by two teachers at the top of their game. Jo and Mel have produced a book that avoids empty preaching and instead offers relevant signposting for the hard-working teacher of today. An important addition to the primary teacher's bookshelf.

Hywel Roberts, travelling teacher, curriculum imagineer and author of *Oops! Helping Children Learn Accidentally*

What makes *Making Every Primary Lesson Count* special is the way it is rooted in theory yet packed full of practical examples. Drawing on their extensive first-hand experience, Jo and Mel show how teachers can turn evidence-based approaches into everyday classroom practice and demonstrate that great teaching isn't about tricks or gimmicks – it's about applying a set of core principles consistently well.

Regardless of whether they are NQTs taking their first steps into the classroom or experienced professionals refining their skills, this book will help all teachers take their practice to the next level.

James Bowen, Director, NAHT Edge

Jo and Mel have done a great job of bringing together research and practice for primary teachers. Each chapter contains useful strategies for creating a more effective learning environment, making good use of the best theory and research without ever forgetting that primary teaching is essentially about the relationships between teachers and their students in the classroom. New teachers will find it a great source of ideas for tackling the key aspects of great teaching, and more experienced teachers will recognise much and pick up a few new ideas along the way.

Michael Tidd, Head Teacher, Medmerry Primary School

Making Every Primary Lesson Count is a highly accessible, practical book for primary teachers which makes constant reference to relevant, current and powerful research evidence.

Its framework provides an essential underpinning of what matters most: challenge, explanation, modelling, deliberate practice, questioning and feedback. The authors have taken all that we currently know about children's learning and woven it into highly practical strategies. Each chapter begins with two real-life scenarios which are then fully analysed and developed. We are not only shown how key research informs us of how we need to teach, but are also given a range of well-sourced practical strategies and ideas.

Several threads run through the writing: the ethos of a growth mindset and the importance of struggle; the framework of formative assessment; high expectations for all with no false ceilings; and the need for clarity, practice and modelling. These ideas, if followed, will go a long way towards helping teachers, as the authors say, "guide children towards independence".

Shirley Clarke, formative assessment expert,
Associate, UCL Institute of Education

Filled with relevant anecdotes and practical examples, *Making Every Primary Lesson Count* explains in detail how to get the very best from every pupil in your care and makes you reflect on the visible difference you can make as a teacher.

Now needed more than ever, this important book will help transform lessons from being dry and functional to serving an actual purpose.

Stephen Lockyer, Enrichment Leader,
Lumen Learning Trust

Using the familiar format of *Making Every Lesson Count*, Jo and Mel have brought a practical wisdom, rooted in primary classroom practice and experience, to this excellent book. A teaching manual full of invaluable guidance for primary practitioners, the values of excellence and growth have been exemplified in each chapter.

Whether you are beginning your teaching career or looking to review and renew your practice, this book will help, support and challenge you in equal measure. Keep it to hand rather than at the back of your teacher's cupboard.

Stephen Tierney, author of *Liminal Leadership*

Making Every Primary Lesson Count is a boon for all those interested in honing their classroom skills by finding out more about the science of pedagogy. It uses key research to produce a range of practical tips and ideas which have been used effectively in school settings.

This book is both engaging and highly readable.

Will Ryan, primary education consultant,
trainer and author

Making every primary lesson count

*Six principles to support great
teaching and learning*

Jo Payne and Mel Scott

Edited by Shaun Allison and Andy Tharby

Crown House Publishing Limited
www.crownhouse.co.uk

First published by

Crown House Publishing Limited
Crown Buildings, Bancyfelin, Carmarthen, Wales, SA33 5ND, UK
www.crownhouse.co.uk

and

Crown House Publishing Company LLC
PO Box 2223, Williston, VT 05495, USA
www.crownhousepublishing.com

British Library Cataloguing-in-Publication Data

A catalogue entry for this book is available from the British Library.

Print ISBN 978-178583181-2
Mobi ISBN 978-178583257-4
ePub ISBN 978-178583258-1
ePDF ISBN 978-178583259-8

LCCN 2017942460

Printed and bound in the UK by
Gomer Press, Llandysul, Ceredigion

Acknowledgements

We would like to thank our amazing colleagues and pupils at Vale School, both past and present, who have provided the inspiration for this book. Particular thanks must go to our head teacher, Martin Garratt, for his support, encouragement and unwavering commitment to the pursuit of excellence.

Jo: I would like to thank my family, who have been encouraging and supportive throughout this process. My mother, Janet Sharp, has inspired my understanding, views and knowledge of education and is greatly responsible for my passion for and enjoyment of teaching. I am particularly grateful to my husband, Matt, who has been incredibly patient during the writing of this book; the process was made easier because of his continuing care and love.

Mel: I would like to thank my partner, Nicholas, for allowing me the time and space to write and for providing invaluable support. I would also like to thank my children, Daisy and Oscar – your belief in me has been my greatest inspiration and I am so very proud of you both. Most of all, I would like to thank my wonderful parents, David and Dorothy. Over the years, you have given both your time and love so generously.

Contents

Introduction

A primary teacher's cupboard can tell many tales: items kept for years after they cease to be part of the curriculum can be unearthed from its depths. After all, they may be needed again. Some objects in the cupboard have never been used: those heavily discounted wooden flowers – surely they hold too much potential to be thrown out? You can never be entirely sure what is stored in The Cupboard until the time comes to reorganise it, once and for all.

Both of us have recently experienced the need to sort through the mysterious items in our cupboards. Mel moved classrooms and, despite having relocated many times and held on to the entire contents – including those resources lurking at the back which had been passed on by previous guardians – this time she decided that a full-scale de-clutter was required. Jo needed to locate her copy of a storybook that she knew would be perfect for teaching some English lessons on imperative verbs; she knew it was somewhere in The Cupboard. Many items were found which are completely irrelevant to what happens in our classrooms now, each with its own tale to tell.

We discovered display resources and activity sheets for literacy and numeracy lessons, now called English and mathematics in the new national curriculum. These were not replaced on the shelves. Alongside them were Velcro ability-group signs for various subjects, dating back to when we first started teaching. We have long since moved away from grouping children by ability so they were added to the growing collection of discarded items. Boxes of redundant test papers were found, including one or two papers stretching back to the year Jo took her own Year 6 SATs! Needless to say, they weren't in line with the current curriculum so were no longer needed. We also found various leaflets, booklets and publications from long-closed government bodies, kept for reference but gathering dust.

Once our cupboards were well-organised and stripped back to the essentials, it led us to consider what would be left if we went through the same exercise with our teaching. Those who have been in the profession for just a few years will have already witnessed a sea change in what constitutes a good lesson and in how teachers should make assessments. Others, who have been teaching for longer, will have observed many transformations, variations and amendments – a constantly changing cycle. We decided that good practice remains at the heart of this ever-changing profession.

In recent years, schools have been given a greater degree of autonomy over what they choose to teach and how they assess pupils. Alongside this, Ofsted have stopped grading individual lessons. Teachers have more freedom in class than they've had for over a decade, and can develop their teaching in a way that suits them, their schools and their pupils. Analysis of PISA results suggests that "when autonomy and accountability are intelligently combined, they tend to be associated with better student performance".[1] So, in this current climate of change and autonomy, in which we strive hard to enable our pupils to succeed, what does good practice look like?

In *Making Every Lesson Count*, Shaun Allison and Andy Tharby point out that these changes are welcome but daunting. They ask, "If we are to make every lesson count, what simple and manageable actions have the greatest impact on learning?"[2] In this book, we have embraced the ethos and six evidence-informed pedagogical principles identified by Allison and Tharby and applied them to the primary context. These principles – challenge, explanation, modelling, practice, feedback and questioning – lie at the heart of good practice and successful teaching. We are not offering quick fixes or gimmicks, instead we hope that new and experienced teachers alike will benefit from our exploration of how attending to the small details can enhance practice and create a rich learning environment.

Everything that follows in this book is underpinned by two values: *excellence* and *growth*. Ron Berger, in *An Ethic of Excellence*, suggests that, regardless of their family background, abilities or disabilities, he wants the same thing for all his pupils: to give them the chance to be excellent – to create work of which they are proud and which is worthy of that pride.[3] Having high expectations of pupils is simply the starting point; it is the culture within a school that encourages and supports pupils to succeed. Berger recommends that schools "consciously shape" the culture so that academic effort, caring about your work and taking pride in drafting, redrafting and creating an excellent final piece of work becomes the norm.

1 See Miyako Ikeda, School Autonomy and Accountability: Are They Related to Student Performance? *PISA in Focus* 9 (Paris: OECD, 2011). Available at: http://www.oecd.org/pisa/pisaproducts/pisainfocus/48910490.pdf, p. 1.

2 Shaun Allison and Andy Tharby, *Making Every Lesson Count: Six Principles to Support Great Teaching and Learning* (Carmarthen: Crown House Publishing, 2015), p. 2.

3 Ron Berger, *An Ethic of Excellence: Building a Culture of Craftsmanship with Students* (Portsmouth, NH: Heinemann, 2003), p. 6.

Encouraging children to aim for excellence links to Stanford University psychologist Carol Dweck's ideas about mindset. Dweck's research has led her to believe that people's opinions about themselves have a profound influence on their lives.[4] She has identified two mindsets that human beings adopt when faced with an obstacle or challenge: a *fixed mindset* or a *growth mindset*. Those who display a fixed mindset believe that abilities and personal qualities are carved in stone. They engage in activities when they are confident of success and avoid situations in which they may fail. Others, demonstrating a growth mindset, know that qualities such as intellectual ability can be developed through effort. In other words, with a fixed mindset, if a child doesn't succeed, they may blame it on their natural ability – for example, claiming they have always been a poor speller and accepting this as a fact rather than seeking to improve. Alternatively, those with a growth mindset strive to learn from their mistakes, aiming to do better next time. They regard failing as an opportunity to learn. Dweck has since cautioned that we are all a mixture of both mindsets, but recognising when we, and our pupils, are demonstrating the traits of a fixed mindset will help us to engage in the struggle to succeed. For example, if a child struggles to begin a piece of writing, helping that child to appreciate how they are feeling, and how they can move forward, will hopefully lead them to recognise this stage on another occasion and provide them with a strategy for overcoming this.

A school ethos which gives pupils the opportunity to work hard and aim for excellence can only flourish when great teaching is taking place every day in the classroom. In this book, we will share with you what the research evidence suggests, what we have learned from inspirational teaching colleagues at our school and, above all, what we continue to learn from our day-to-day experiences as classroom teachers.

---

4 Carol S. Dweck, *Mindset: How You Can Fulfil Your Potential* (London: Robinson, 2006).

We have tackled the same interrelated pedagogical principles as discussed in *Making Every Lesson Count*, which can be implemented in different year groups, subjects and topics as appropriate. The principles work as follows:

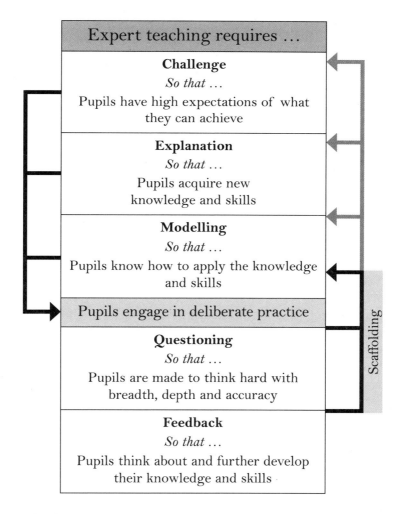

The focus of Chapter 1 is *challenge*. This chapter evaluates how high expectations and struggle allow pupils to move beyond what they can do now.

In Chapter 2, on *explanation*, we consider how best to convey the concepts we are teaching to our pupils. Teacher talk and concrete, clear examples are key, so these are discussed in detail.

We move on to *modelling* in Chapter 3. This involves discussing and dissecting a piece of work, or creating an exemplar and verbalising the thought process required.

Pupils must engage in *practice* in order to ensure that learning is embedded effectively. This will be the focus for Chapter 4.

Without *feedback*, teachers and pupils have nothing to guide them on the right path. Chapter 5 ponders the cycle through which teachers give feedback to children about their work and receive feedback to inform future learning.

Like explanation, *questioning* is a skilful art which has a range of purposes. In Chapter 6 we review how teachers can use questions to test for misconceptions, solidify understanding and promote deeper thought.

Within the context of a solid foundation of effective classroom management and strong relationships between adults and pupils, these six principles are designed to help you guide your children towards independence. They are not designed to be a cycle which is adhered to in each lesson or topic. Rather, the principles are interwoven throughout teaching sequences and can be called upon when necessary. Sometimes, two principles can be most effective when adopted simultaneously – for example, using questioning to gain feedback about a child's learning or using modelling to support an explanation.

Each chapter begins with two fictional scenarios which are rooted in situations primary teachers typically encounter. We then consider the principle – what it is and why it matters – before explaining some strategies that can be employed in day-to-day practice. Each chapter concludes with a list of reflective questions. Hopefully you will find these useful to review your implementation of each principle as you are preparing for and reflecting on lessons, and hopefully they will enable you to use planning, teaching and assessment time effectively to ensure the best learning outcomes for your pupils.

We have already mentioned that we believe that at the heart of this ever-changing profession lies good practice based on two key values: we hope this book will inspire you to develop a culture of growth and excellence with your pupils.

Chapter 1
Challenge

Elisa – the circle

When Elisa moved out of Early Years, her Year 1 teacher put her in the Circles group for maths. She spent the year completing fairly easy work and she often had the support of a teaching assistant to do this. As she moved into Year 2, she was, once again, placed on the Circles table. Elisa no longer wondered what she must do to get into the Triangles group and had stopped trying to aim for it. Now she is starting Year 6 and is concerned that she will still be seated with the Circles. On her first day of term, Elisa's new teacher gives each child a sticky note and asks them to write down one thing that they really wish their new teacher knew about them. Elisa writes, "I would like to be on the Hexagons table, like my sister was, because I am clever."

Ben's beeline for help

Year 3 pupil Ben relied on support. In fact, he would make a beeline for any teaching assistant entering the classroom and ask them to work with him. He was also very reward hungry. The only way to encourage him to produce any work or follow a task was to dangle the carrot of a sticker or house points.

Although this served the purpose of enticing him to engage with a task, it taught Ben that it was the outcome that mattered rather than the process. This also meant that he expected an extrinsic reward for whatever he produced, no matter the quality.

Challenge – What It Is and Why It Matters

Challenge gives pupils the opportunity to stretch themselves and encourages them to believe that hard work and perseverance will lead to progress. Within the classroom, this means setting challenging targets that all pupils have the opportunity to access and work that probes the pupils' thinking, enabling them to learn in greater depth. Malcolm Gladwell observes in *Outliers* that, as a society, we "cling to the idea that success is a simple function of individual merit".[1] He suggests that we are too much in awe of successful individuals and far too dismissive of those who fail. Society encourages competitiveness and comparison from the very start of life, from parents who compare Apgar scores (a simple test to determine how ready a newborn is to meet the world) to those who praise toddlers for ability rather than effort: "You're *so* clever!"

Dweck's research into mindsets has found that as soon as children become able to evaluate themselves, some of them become afraid of challenges. They become worried about how their intelligence will be perceived if they do not succeed. Elisa knows that 'clever' people should always succeed and is already, at the age of 10, comparing herself unfavourably with a sibling. Elisa needs to be encouraged to change her mindset: to believe that the success she craves can be developed through effort, stretching herself, taking on more

---

1 Malcolm Gladwell, *Outliers: The Story of Success* (London: Penguin, 2008), p. 33.

challenging work and accepting that failure may be a painful part of the struggle – but one from which she can learn. As Dweck points out, "It's not about immediate perfection. It's about learning something over time: confronting a challenge and making progress."[2]

A careful balance needs to be struck – as in the figure below. As Allison and Tharby explain, "While we want to move students out of their comfort zone into the struggle zone, we also need to ensure that we do not push them so far that they end up in the panic zone."[3] The skill of the teacher is in pushing pupils just far enough so that they are engaging with worthwhile and productive struggle.

Comfort zone	Struggle zone	Panic zone
Low challenge. Low stress. Limited thinking. Limited learning.	High challenge. Low stress. Thinking required. Effective learning.	Very high challenge. High stress. Cognitive overload. Limited learning.

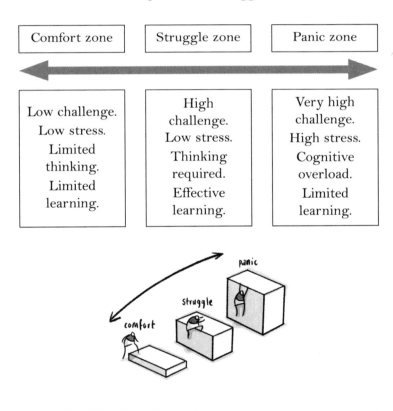

---

2 Dweck, *Mindset*, p. 24.
3 Allison and Tharby, *Making Every Lesson Count*, p. 16.

As teachers, we need to do more than just talk about growth mindset in order to encourage pupils. The phrasing of our feedback and the way we approach errors and setbacks can help pupils on their own journey to acquiring the traits of a growth mindset. Since publishing her research, Dweck has cautioned about the creation of false growth mindsets. We should not be banning the fixed mindset from our class-rooms because it is important to acknowledge that "(1) we're all a mixture of fixed and growth mindsets, (2) we will prob-ably always be, and (3) if we want to move closer to a growth mindset in our thoughts and practices, we need to stay in touch with our fixed-mindset thoughts and deeds".[4] Dweck advocates watching out for our fixed mindset triggers. This is true of ourselves as teachers as well as of our pupils. Once we recognise these triggers, both ours and our pupils', be it anxiety when facing a setback or reluctance to accept criti-cism, we are better able to accept them and work through them.

So, how do we challenge all children in the class and help them to develop the traits of a growth mindset? Setting high expectations for all pupils regardless of their starting point will help to ensure that the challenge is kept high. Your response to individuals and the ways in which they are supported to reach these high standards will vary according to the needs of each pupil. The following figure demon-strates Allison and Tharby's solution to the problem of ensuring that needs are met yet challenge is kept high.

---

4   Carol S. Dweck, Carol Dweck Revisits the 'Growth Mindset', *Education Week* (22 September 2015). Available at: www.edweek.org/ew/articles/2015/09/23/carol-dweck-revisits-the-growth-mindset.html.

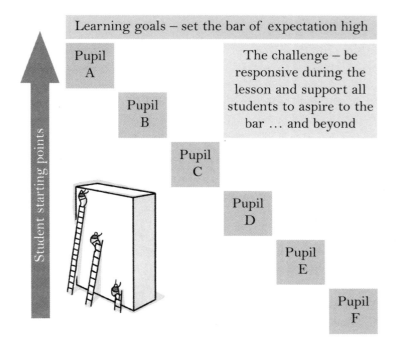

Our colleague, Year 3 teacher Sam Blaker, demonstrated these high expectations when working with Ben, mentioned in the second scenario. The class had been studying Roald Dahl's *The Twits* and discovered that Mrs Twit had become ugly due to her having ugly thoughts. The class were engaged in writing some good thoughts to prevent such hideousness! As usual, Ben had written the bare minimum and expected this to be acceptable. He demonstrated the traits of having a fixed mindset. Sam was determined to help Ben change his mindset. This was the conversation that ensued:

Sam: Well done for writing your thoughts on your own. I see you've written "Going to Spain". That sounds nice. Why does going to Spain make you happy?

Ben (in a low growly voice, looking away and turning his back on her): *Why should I tell you?*

Sam: Because I was interested and wanted to help you make your writing even better. But if you wish to leave it like that, then that's fine.

(She turned to walk away.)

Ben: Okay, okay, I'll tell you!

He then proceeded to tell her how the hotel where he stays has a great swimming pool and that it cools you down when it is "super-hot". Sam then suggested ideas about how he could extend his existing sentence with 'because' and supported him accordingly. Once he had done this she praised him for improving his work and for accepting advice, not for the final outcome.

Over the next term, she continued to praise Ben for his independent efforts (though he still liked to have an adult with him to talk through and model ideas) and always found an element on which to give positive feedback, before offering suggestions for improvement. Slowly Ben's attitude towards his learning changed. He realised that it was good to find things to change, it was good to borrow brilliance from others, it was good to ask for advice and it was good to wo independently – that is what Mrs Blaker liked. He had learned to become more of an enthusiastic, resilient, determined and successful learner.

The following strategies guide you through some practical ideas that can be used to help you challenge your pupils as well as yourself.

1. Be Precise

How do I cultivate a classroom culture of challenge through the routines and language I use?

Establishing efficient routines is key in primary education, beginning in the Early Years classroom – from where to hang their coats, how to sit on the carpet and when to look at the teacher to exactly which items of clothing to remove when changing for PE and how to zip their coats at the end of the day! Early Years practitioners are experts at establishing good practice through frequent repetition and modelling – for example, reinforcing expectations through role play with a teaching assistant. The way the adults interact in the classroom reinforces the high expectations for behaviour and social interaction. Some children begin their schooling with limited or delayed speech, so it is vital that f school is modelled consistently so that all the expectations.

1 progress through Key Stages 1 and 2, it is bed routines so the children are clear about what is expected in the classroom and time is not wasted during transition from one lesson to the next. It is a valuable use of time at the beginning of the year to be precise about classroom routines and to practise these repeatedly – handing out books, being prepared with the right equipment, knowing where to place homework, understanding the standard of presentation expected. Set a challenge at the start of the year and repeat at the beginning of each term to time how quickly a routine can be carried out. Doug Lemov, in *Teach Like a Champion*, refers to this as "engineering efficiency".[5] He recommends explicitly teaching children the simplest and fastest procedure for executing key classroom tasks, then practising so that executing it becomes a habit. Keep routines simple and quick to carry out, using set, short phrases. Allowing the children to take responsibility for organising the smooth transition from one lesson to the next will free you to begin the lesson at a good pace.

Having clear procedures indicates what is valued by the school. Teachers at Michaela Community School spend seven days at the beginning of Year 7 teaching children how to meet the high standards for responsibility, punctuality and politeness, so the expectations are understood and the children are empowered by this culture of high standards.[6] The time gained through effective routines and efficient transitions justifies making this a crucial part of setting up a classroom.

The language of school should not only be used by the teacher for establishing routines. Children can be encouraged

---

5   Doug Lemov, *Teach Like a Champion 2.0: 62 Techniques That Put Students on the Path to College* (San Francisco, CA: Jossey-Bass, 2015), p. 361.
6   See Joe Kirby, No Excuses: High Standards, High Support, *Pragmatic Education* (10 December 2016). Available at: https://pragmaticreform. wordpress.com/2016/12/10/no-excuses-high-standards-high-support/.

to respond to questions in class with language that is appropriate and to recognise that the clarity of vocabulary used to communicate ideas is immensely important. It can be pointed out that we all speak differently in different situations, but that articulating answers using more formal language is good practice for writing. Consider the difference between the following two exchanges during a whole-class reading session:

Teacher: When does Rafael begin to feel nervous?

Bethany: When he, like, enters the cave-thingy.

Teacher: Yes, Rafael begins to feel nervous when he enters the cavern.

Teacher: When does Rafael begin to feel nervous?

Bethany: When he, like, enters the cave-thingy.

Teacher: Whole sentence, precise language please.

Bethany: Rafael begins to feel nervous when he enters the cavern.

Teacher: Thank you, Bethany.

In the first example, although the teacher models the correct way to respond to the question, she is sending a message to Bethany that her answer is acceptable. The second example demands that the child works harder than the teacher. With a clear and polite instruction, the teacher expects the child to rephrase her answer using a complete sentence and more formal language. The teacher then shows that she values the improvement by thanking her.

If Bethany were unable or only partially able to improve her first sentence, it would be a good idea to ask a peer to assist in improving it. Once a good model has been created, the teacher can ask Bethany to repeat the improved sentence. Resist the urge to accept a 'good enough' answer because 'there is a lot to cover in the lesson and time is precious'. It may feel as if a lot of time is being spent on one response, but orally rehearsing an answer will help that child – and others listening who struggle to put their ideas into words – to use and become familiar with formal language structures. In this way, pupils are far more likely to be able to frame a written response correctly.

Mel introduced the idea of using formal language in the classroom by linking it with the book that her Year 6 class were reading, *The Giver* by Lois Lowry. In the strictly controlled society featured in *The Giver*, members of the community must speak with a "precision of language". This theme led to many in-depth discussions about the meaning of words and how we communicate, and the class decided to attempt to eliminate 'well' and 'like' and other imprecise phrases from their answers. They enjoyed monitoring each other's responses, which resulted in the added benefit of encouraging them to focus on their peers' answers.

2. One Challenging Learning Objective for All

How can I encourage all children to aim high?

At some point, many of us will have designed a lesson, or a series of lessons, based on learning objectives with differentiated outcomes (using, for instance, 'must, should, could' or 'all, most, some'), unintentionally setting a glass ceiling for some children.

For example, the success criteria for writing a historical narrative may have looked like this:

Must:

◊ Write in first-person narrative

◊ Include historical facts

◊ Use descriptive language

Should:

◊ Maintain your point of view

◊ Use historical vocabulary

◊ Include direct speech

Could:

◊ Begin with a flashback

◊ Use emotive language

For some children, this sends the message either that we do not expect a lot from them or that it is acceptable not to aim high. We prefer to offer all pupils the opportunity to reach as high as they can. The success criteria could be represented as follows:

Success criteria

◊ Write in first-person narrative

◊ Maintain your point of view

◊ Include historical facts

◊ Use historical vocabulary

◊ Use descriptive language

◊ Appeal to the senses and emotions

◊ Consider beginning with a flashback

By setting one learning objective that demonstrates high expectations, we are challenging ourselves as well as the children. A clear message is sent to the pupils that all are expected to aim high and we, as teachers, are challenged to find ways to support and encourage all children to succeed. The top-down planning approach enables teachers to experiment with strategies to raise the achievement of those who typically may not have been expected to attain more than the 'must' or 'all' sections of the criteria.

When planning a series of lessons, consider using this approach:

1   Identify the top achieving child in the class and plan your lesson as if the whole class were working at this level.

2   Create resources and tasks that will challenge this child at the appropriate level.

3   Consider how to provide scaffolds for other members of the class, such as prompts (either written or verbal), word banks, key questions or concrete resources.

Children are often good at assessing the level of support that they require, but helpful hints from the teacher can encourage them to challenge themselves further or seek support as appropriate. Effective scaffolding, which enables all children to aim high, will help to create a culture of success.

3. Elevate the Standard

How do I let the children know what I expect from them?

Across all subjects, it is important for the children to understand what you are hoping they will accomplish. With this in mind, it can be useful to begin with the outcome and work backwards, to ask: for this to be successful, what is required? All children, regardless of their starting point, need to be encouraged to aim for the highest standard possible. How do you show them what this looks like?

1   Share completed pieces of work that serve to benchmark brilliance. This could be examples of the same piece of work from a previous cohort, examples from similar pieces of work which display transferable skills or examples of work from children in an older year group. Children enjoy the challenge of aiming for a standard set by older pupils.

2   Mix it up. Don't begin each unit of work in the same way – occasionally show the children a piece of work that doesn't reach the high standard you expect. After some practice, they will undoubtedly be able to let you know that this falls short of the standard they expect to be shown and in what ways it needs to be improved.

3   Start a school blog where children are nominated by their teachers to have their work posted. The children enjoy having their work seen and recognised by a wider community.

Mel shared completed pieces of work with her Year 6 pupils to challenge them to raise their expectations of their own capabilities in writing. Taking a thematic approach to writing, the children spent six weeks learning through the study of a battle in Ancient Greece: the Battle of Marathon. The unit included writing a persuasive speech and a strategic battle plan and culminated in a narrative written from an eyewitness perspective. In order to set the bar high, the children were shown two openings to a narrative based on the Battle of Hastings written by able Year 7 students (from when Vale School was a first and middle school). An entire lesson was spent reading, deconstructing and comparing the two openings before discussing the impact of language choices and overall effect. The children chose which piece of work they admired the most (they were evenly divided) and annotated it with comments on figurative language, sentence structure and how punctuation was used for dramatic effect. The children then drew on these excellent models to help them aim high.

Helen Cooper, a colleague who teaches art throughout Key Stage 2, keeps a book of examples of previous work, one for each year group. The exemplars not only demonstrate excellence of outcome but also show effort and progress. She talks to her pupils about the children who produced the work, describing the challenges they faced and the struggle they engaged in, and describes how they overcame these challenges to produce their artwork. She believes that it is important for children to recognise that they will not have identical outcomes, but they are more likely to achieve success if they can be inspired by what has been achieved by others. Some children demonstrate natural vision, while others benefit from being shown what is possible, and in this way discover, with guidance, what they are capable of achieving. For example, Year 6 pupils study the artist Hundertwasser and are inspired both by the works of the artist and the examples of pupils' work that are shared with them.

4. One Set of Success Criteria for All

Should I differentiate the task or the success criteria?

If you are encouraging all children to aim high, then the answer to this question is neither. If you believe that hard work, determination and perseverance will generate success, why would you give some children a simpler task, direct some children towards only achieving part of the success criteria or allow children to 'choose' a level of challenge? How you respond to needs as they arise in class and support individuals will differ, but all should be encouraged to aspire to the same standard of excellence.

It is now widely accepted that learning intentions should be shared with the children; in order for the children to know how to meet these intentions, success criteria can provide valuable guidance. However, there are a variety of ways in which success criteria can be employed. To support developing resilience and aiming high, consider moving away from using 'must, should, could' or 'all, most, some', which indicates levels of differentiation, and instead move towards one set of success criteria for all, presented in a list, table or grid. At times, you will want to simply present the success criteria to the children. At others, you may wish to develop the success criteria with the children. However, Dylan Wiliam points out that developing success criteria with children "is most definitely not a democratic process".[7] The advantage is in encouraging ownership of the success criteria by involving the children in their creation, but the teacher is always in the privileged position of being able to direct the process.

5. Personal Challenge

How do I challenge each individual?

You are aiming for pupils to be working just outside their comfort zone in order to make the most of the opportunities to develop their knowledge and skills. How do we ensure that this is happening? In the primary setting, we have the advantage of having an in-depth knowledge of the individual children in our class – we are with them five hours a day, five days a week. We chat to them, know who their friends are and what they did at the weekend, and crucially we know where they are with their learning and what their next steps need to be. The most effective way to feed back to children is face to face during the lesson.

Feedback is discussed in detail in Chapter 5, but it is worth noting here that giving less written feedback in individual books and instead allowing yourself time to focus on planning for how to move individual children forward will reap rewards. Some common errors and misconceptions can be addressed with timely whole-class feedback and the use of a visualiser: "Many of us have described the process of separating the mixture well but are struggling with evaluating

---

7   Dylan Wiliam, *Embedded Formative Assessment* (Bloomington, IN: Solution Tree Press, 2011), p. 59.

our methods. Let's look at why Rachel's was so good." The children can then improve their work having critiqued a good model. You can also note down comments to discuss with individuals during the next lesson, such as reminding them to refer to their plan, to use the word bank provided to extend their vocabulary or to think about a whole sentence in their head before writing it.

Reading the children's work without pausing to give detailed feedback in each book – potentially reducing the process from three hours to thirty minutes – also allows you to identify those children who have struggled with the task or are not making the progress that you would have expected. You can gather them into a focus group during the next session so that you can ensure they are challenged and supported appropriately. If you have additional adult support in the classroom, rotate the groups that you work with and don't always offer support to the same children. All the children need to know that they cannot rely on adult support and that they are expected to aim high and work independently. Focused time with a small, regularly changing group of children enables you to offer support and direct challenge to a greater number of individuals.

To recap, to make this process manageable and to ensure that over the course of a few sessions or weeks each child is personally challenged, shift the focus from lengthy marking sessions in books to:

♦ Planning timely whole-class feedback on common misconceptions.

♦ Planning well-directed suggestions/reminders for individuals to keep them on track.

♦ Identifying individuals who would benefit from targeted support, working with you or another adult in class.

6. Value Excellence

How can I show children that I value excellence?

Carol Dweck's research has shown that when children adopt a growth mindset they have a greater ability to motivate themselves, value what they are doing more and achieve greater success; this, in turn, can inspire others. Children with a fixed mindset can be reluctant to push themselves out of their comfort zone to engage with a truly challenging task. They believe that they shouldn't have to put in effort in order to achieve, and worry about failure and how this will be perceived. Encouraging children to develop a growth mindset needs to be embedded in the ethos of the school. So how can you demonstrate that having the right attitude towards exerting effort and learning from setbacks is valued as an important factor in achieving excellence?

Durrington High School, inspired by Pete Jones of Les Quennevais School, Jersey, has transformed an area of the school into a 'gallery of excellence'. This sets the standard of expectation high, provides a reference point for pupils and celebrates quality work. The work is mounted in frames which serves to show that it is highly valued.

At Vale School, we wanted to take this idea and transform it into our own model for how we value excellence in a primary setting. To embed the idea of growth mindset, each year group – from Early Years to Year 6 – has a character that embodies the characteristics of a child with a growth mindset – for example, Have a Go Flamingo, Try it Tiger or Step up Star – and the children are encouraged to emulate these characters. A prominent area in the school displays our 'aiming for excellence' gallery, and in this space it is our intention not just to value and display excellent examples of finished work. We also want to celebrate a piece of work from initial plan, through draft and improvement stages, to the completed successful piece of work or a series of pieces that demonstrate resilience and determination to succeed. In this way, we can value the process, resilience and grit demonstrated. In addition, we can show that we recognise the work of all pupils rather than just a small group of high-performing individuals. The examples of work are changed on a termly basis, featuring a different subject or theme each term.

This idea can be extended to the classroom, but rather than being termly, displays of examples of excellent work can be reactive and timely. Examples of excellent work do not need to be copied into 'best' and double-mounted on card before being displayed. If a child has written a great story opening or persevered with a maths problem, photocopy it and have it on display before the next lesson. The child will appreciate seeing such a recent effort displayed, and other children will benefit from the good model or the reminder that being resilient can lead to success. To illustrate this, Martin Garratt, the head teacher at Vale School, shares *The Dot* by Peter H. Reynolds with pupils.[8] This simple yet inspirational

8   Peter H. Reynolds, *The Dot* (London: Walker Books, 2004).

story details the journey taken by a pupil who believes she cannot draw. With encouraging support from a teacher, resilience and practice, she discovers her ability to succeed.

Your reward system can also help to raise the level of challenge. Our Year 3 pupils are rewarded with 'Try it Tiger' stickers when they have demonstrated perseverance and several children in Year 6 are rewarded each week for having stepped up and demonstrated a growth mindset. They recognise that their 'turn' to be the Step up Star isn't automatic, but that they actively have to propel themselves out of their comfort zone to be awarded this accolade.

Invite stakeholders into the school – governors, parents and the wider community – to view a gallery of work. This could be an art exhibition, a museum exhibition on a particular theme (we set up a Second World War museum with the children in the role of experts) or an opportunity to hear the pupils reading their own poetry aloud. It is important for the children to see their work being valued in different ways.

7. Consider the Audience

Can a real-life audience for a task improve pupil outcomes?

When aiming to give purpose to children's work, it is worth considering the power of a real audience – other than their teacher – and the impact this can have in encouraging them to take responsibility for their own learning. When children work towards an end product to share with an authentic audience, it makes them realise that quality genuinely matters and that people care about the outcome and want them to succeed. Therefore, they don't want to let down their well-wishers.

Ron Berger's hierarchy of audience (shown on page 30) demonstrates that the knowledge that their work is real and important is powerful in raising pupils' motivation and engagement.[9]

The key is to harness the enthusiasm that this work generates so that it contributes to developing a strong ethos and work ethic in the classroom.

Here are a few ideas to consider:

♦ Tie in with current events:

　◊ Children in the Early Years painted pictures of the Queen in response to the release of the Queen's 90th birthday portrait and sent them to Buckingham Palace. It is always exciting to receive a reply!

　◊ Year 5 joined the 8,600 schools involved in an exciting experiment with astronaut Tim Peake to investigate whether seeds of the salad plant rocket which had been in space for six months would grow as well as those that had remained on Earth.

♦ Connect with a favourite author:

　◊ Early Years pupils wrote letters to Julia Donaldson inviting her to come to their 'Scarecrows' Wedding'

9　Figure adapted from Ron Berger, Leah Rugen and Libby Woodfin, *Leaders of Their Own Learning: Transforming Schools through Student-Engaged Assessment* (San Francisco, CA: Jossey-Bass, 2014), p. 216.

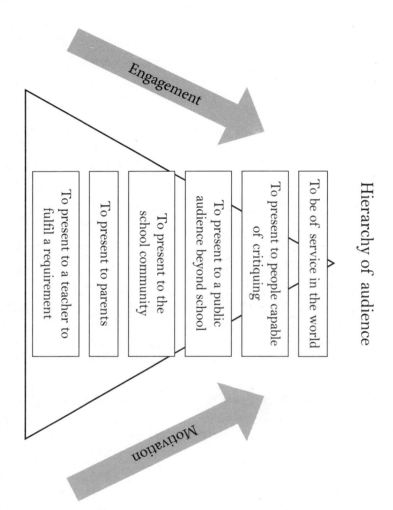

and were delighted to receive a reply (even though Julia was unable to attend!).

♦ Respond to first-hand experience:

◊ Year 1 children wrote letters to the local fire brigade following a safety demonstration on the school playground.

◊ Children across the school wrote thank-you letters to our parent–teacher association which had provided wet-play games and a company that had donated hundreds of books to the school.

♦ Link with the wider school community:

◊ Year 6 pupils used their food technology skills to design and test recipes for a cafe. They rose to the challenge of budgeting, writing invitations, designing a logo and decorating a classroom. Each class ran their cafe (attended by parents, governors and teachers) for two hours and gained a valuable insight into working life and an immense sense of achievement from coping when things didn't go quite to plan! Their customers were then invited to comment on the quality of the food and service.

◊ At the end of each academic year, children from each year group spend time reflecting on their work, choosing several pieces from across the curriculum and preparing to present their work to their parents, explaining how these pieces demonstrate the progress they have made.

♦ Link with the local community:

◊ Year 2 children designed and made cakes. To give their ideas a focus, they were asked to generate suggestions for cakes that could be sold at a local cafe. The ideas were presented to the cafe's owners, who responded by selecting their favourite ones.

◊ The local shopping parade holds an annual Christmas market and the pavement is lined with festive stalls. Year 4 became involved by designing and making cards, decorations and gifts. They took great pride in calculating the costings, maintaining quality control and ultimately selling their wares on their market stall.

◊ The school gardening club collaborated with the local residents' association to plant new trees in the school grounds.

◊ When Vale School was a first and middle school, to tie in with Year 7's theme of national parks, they took part in the Annual Schools Exhibition at the Towner Art Gallery in Eastbourne, which that year was run in partnership with Learning Through Landscapes and the South Downs National Park. A different theme is given to schools every year and each school chooses how to respond.

8. Jack of All Trades, Master of Many

How can I extend my subject knowledge across the breadth of the primary curriculum?

The craft of the primary teacher has developed in a generalist way. As a result, the demands on the subject knowledge of primary teachers are immense. Along with clear learning objectives, well-structured lessons and effective questioning skills, a teacher's subject knowledge is an essential factor in good teaching. This enables us to tackle misconceptions and field more probing questions, as well as ensuring that a high level of challenge is set for all pupils.

Some teachers within the primary environment may have specialised in how children in a particular age group learn, while others may have a subject specialism. How do we ensure that, as busy professionals, we can equip ourselves with the knowledge and expertise to meet the demands of the entire breadth of the primary curriculum? A collaborative, whole-school approach is essential: we need to nurture each other's knowledge. As individuals, we must also recognise the areas where we need extra support and those where we can lend support to others. A 'buddy' system between teachers can be mutually beneficial – focusing on team teaching and advice with planning, especially for subjects such as modern foreign languages or technical aspects of computing. Piloting a task in subjects in which you have less experience before setting it to the children can provide an essential insight into the practical and cognitive difficulties that pupils may face – for example, in a design and technology project to make a moving vehicle. Making the most of the expertise of colleagues will make for more effective lessons.

As a community of professionals, in-house subject-specific training is an important element of continuing professional development. Working in teams to investigate an area and feed back to all staff can be highly effective. It can be helpful to make links with other primary schools and local secondary schools, calling on their know-how and sharing knowledge and good practice. Involving secondary school departments in advising on and helping to plan a unit of work can be especially useful for all involved. Following education groups on social media, such as Twitter, can also enable you to keep up to date with current thinking and practices, develop subject knowledge, make links and share ideas with other teachers. Jo has had many teachers visit her classroom after following her blog posts about how she organises whole-class reading activities. We need to work together to make that powerful link between enhancing our own subject knowledge, and that of others, having high expectations for all pupils and enabling high levels of attainment for our pupils across all subjects.

9. You Choose

How does giving pupils a choice help them to aim high?

Giving pupils choice can be an effective way to motivate and engage them. However, what should be the balance between directed tasks and more open-ended ones? How do you prevent children from making a choice that keeps them in the comfort zone?

Mel initiated a two-day writing challenge with a Year 6 class. The children had the choice of six genres of writing – short stories, play scripts, newspaper reporting, factual reports, biography and balanced argument. In addition, they could choose their subject matter. Almost overwhelmingly, the boys chose to write biographies of famous footballers. They researched, drafted, edited and improved their work with enthusiasm and attention to detail. When asked to reflect on the two-day project, the children wrote about how much they enjoyed the freedom and the time they were given.

The project was repeated twice during the course of the year, with the children being asked to make a different choice of genre each time, thereby challenging themselves further. The freedom gave some children the flexibility to demonstrate their skill in manipulating language and structure, while others started to develop an enjoyment of writing. It was pivotal in changing their attitude towards writing in other situations where the task was more directed. Freedom of choice can be motivational, although it is not often employed. Knowing when to include an element of preference and when to be directive is key.

Reflective Questions

♦ Are expectations clear and routines embedded in my classroom?

♦ How can I encourage perseverance, determination and engagement in productive struggle?

♦ How can I keep my subject knowledge up to date?

♦ Am I actively demonstrating that I value excellence?

♦ Have I considered the power of a real-life audience?

Chapter 2
Explanation

Sofia, the verbose explainer

As a Key Stage 2 teacher, Sofia knows the importance of building children's vocabulary. She is very well-read and well-spoken, and always ensures her sentences are carefully constructed. When introducing something new to her class, she uses unusual and elaborate vocabulary to bulk out her explanations. She believes this will enable her class to deepen their understanding of such words as well as learn the main focus of the lesson. In reality, she is preventing her pupils from accessing the learning by using unnecessary and inaccessible vocabulary.

Richard, the student teacher

Richard is in his final placement of his teacher training and finds himself teaching the Ancient Greeks. He must plan lessons based on their gods and goddesses, the political system that was used and the Battle of Marathon. He generally uses the same structure in each lesson: the children are given lots of information about the topic which they read while making notes on a framework he has provided, before answering some retrieval questions about what they've learned. His next lesson is on the Olympic Games – will he follow the same structure?

Explanation – What It Is and Why It Matters

All six principles in this book are vital to effective teaching, but explanation is the reason formal education began in the first place. Ancient civilisations realised the value of having people who could explain new knowledge and skills to others in a clear and easy-to-understand way, with these early educators unknowingly utilising the other five principles.

Chip and Dan Heath have looked at many cultural ideas which have stuck in people's minds, from branding and advertisements through to political campaigns and charity appeals.[1] As they did so, they discovered that the same six principles were at play. These principles can ensure that a new skill or concept will be embedded for the long term.

1 **Keep it simple.** Focus on the main objective and refrain from adding on extras. If children are learning about negative numbers for the first time, ensure they can count up and down across a zero before teaching them to calculate with positive and negative numbers.

2 **Use the unexpected.** As well as using surprise to aid long-term memory, use it to generate interest in and curiosity for the new content. Show the children a picture of somewhere which has regular sub-zero temperatures and ask them to guess what the temperature would be. The more shocking or unusual the picture, the better. This will raise questions in their minds and give you some information about their understanding of negative numbers.

3 **Refer to the concrete.** Relate the learning focus to concepts which are familiar to the children. If possible, use resources to make it tactile too. For example, refer to the

1 Chip Heath and Dan Heath, *Made to Stick: Why Some Ideas Take Hold and Others Come Unstuck* (London: Arrow Books, 2007).

underground floors in a shopping centre and places below sea level, as well as minus temperatures.

4   **Make it credible.** Ensure the children believe what you are explaining to them and make it easy for them to do so. If need be, show them real examples which they can access. With negative numbers, for example, show the children videos, from countries where the temperature is extremely low, of hot water freezing in the air.

5   **Engage the emotions.** Make the children feel something about the learning. When they feel, they care and when they care, they remember. Picture books, videos and longer texts can help to promote an emotional response from pupils. Using the phrase, "Imagine if ..." engages the children's imagination and can tap into their emotions.

6   **Tell stories.** Stories can give a context to new content, provide knowledge about learning, supply inspiration for actions and help children to appreciate the relevance of what they are learning. The stories could be from books, historical accounts or anecdotes from your own or someone else's life. A story about someone going up and down in a lift, for example, could help the pupils to understand how to add and subtract numbers across a zero.

Build Connections

Very rarely do we teach an entirely new concept. The primary curriculum is cumulative, therefore children should usually have some knowledge from a previous lesson. Even pupils starting school for the first time have had various experiences on which we can draw. Through feedback, teachers must first understand what it is that children already know, so they can then ensure that the introduction of the new concept links to pupils' prior experiences in and out of school. The Heath brothers suggest that teachers should highlight things the children already know when engaging them in a new area of learning, to increase its stickability.[2]

Rounding numbers is a concept children have always found tricky at our school. Each year, there were a group of children who thought 358 rounded to the nearest 10 was 60 or who kept rounding by simply adding 10, so 358 would become 368 when rounded. The Year 4 teachers changed tack and, instead of starting with the new content (rounding), they started with knowledge the children already had (multiples of 10). This was a really useful building block to avoid a common misconception and to embed the understanding that 'nearest 10' means 'nearest multiple of 10'.

---

2   Heath and Heath, *Made to Stick*, p. 92.

The same resources used previously – number lines, online tools and songs – could then be used to explain the concept of rounding with more success.

Explanation versus Modelling

Explanation and modelling often exist simultaneously when introducing new content, especially in practical subjects. When Alison Bullard teaches food technology, she explains the processes required while demonstrating them. When cutting an onion, she revises the three possible grips children could use (claw, bridge or fork secure) and reminds the children to act them out. Through questioning she asks them to consider which one would be most appropriate and why. She then models how to use the fork-secure hold while explaining how and why it is the best technique for the job. She repeats the strategies of explaining, modelling and questioning multiple times in her lessons, as do many other teachers, particularly in practical subjects.

Choose Carefully

A solid explanation is the key to effective teaching. Where Richard, the teacher in the second opening scenario, is falling short is that he's using the same method of explanation in each lesson: reading. Despite children sometimes learning new knowledge by reading around certain subjects, it is inappropriate to use this strategy as a replacement for teacher explanation. Not only would using the same method become tiresome, but it also fails to recognise the importance of discussion, questioning, creativity, empathy and the many other elements which are a part of great teaching.

The ideas in this chapter should be considered carefully for each subject and even each unit within a subject. Although we have found these to be useful across our school, it is, as always, important to consider the needs of your class and adjust any strategies accordingly.

1. Manage Misconceptions

How can I prevent the children from learning new concepts incorrectly?

From misunderstandings of word meanings to unusual beliefs about the number system, it is easy for children to learn something incorrectly. As teachers, part of our role is to identify where these fires start and extinguish them before they burn for too long and the damage is too deep. Experienced teachers have encountered multiple misconceptions in their classrooms and therefore find it easier to predict when children might misunderstand something. New teachers should check common misconceptions with experienced teachers and plan for them.

As with feedback, immediate verbal intervention during a lesson is most effective at preventing the seeds of misconception from sprouting. Medics, particularly those who work at the scenes of emergencies, refer to the 'golden hour' as the time after an accident or incident during which prompt medical treatment is most likely to save a life. Teachers should bear this in mind during their lessons – can you save a child from a lifetime of difficulty? Which children are the ones who readily misunderstand? Is there time to check and correct their understanding in the lesson, preferably soon after the original input? If so, it is certainly worth taking this time, as two minutes spent addressing a fundamental misconception during a lesson could prevent a child from facing difficulty in their future learning.

We have often looked through books after a lesson and found a child whose misconception has led them to repeatedly make the same mistake. In completing two-digit by one-digit multiplication, children sometimes forget their place value knowledge. For example:

---

3 7

x 6

4 2 (7 x 6)

+

1 8 (3 x 6 but it should be 30 x 6, i.e. 180)

6 0 (the correct answer should be 222)

1

---

2. Make Relatable Connections

How can I explain complex ideas in an accessible way?

When starting a new unit of learning, teachers in our school talk to teachers in the year group below to find out what was learned previously and how well the children understood it. We know that starting with what they already understand provides an ideal hook into the new learning; it makes it tangible. This strategy is about making the learning relatable to the children; not just in the sense of their prior learning but in terms of them being human beings who have emotions that we can tap into.

Tell personal anecdotes

Recently retired deputy head teacher Sue Smith is an expert in explaining using stories. Facts are important for learning, but Sue believes that empathy is the hook by which facts can be explained.

Sue begins her explanation of the state of Germany in 1939 with the following sentence: "This story is important to me …" Immediately, her class becomes an audience and the learning has been given a context. They sit in stunned silence as she explains the divisions in the country using a personal anecdote relating to her own family. Most pupils can relate easily to the familial connections Sue mentions, despite the fact that none of them were alive when the events took place.

Primary pupils are highly interested in the lives of their teachers. On learning new information, even if it's just a first name, they are excited and engaged. Telling stories about ourselves, even if we're bending the truth slightly, can give our explanations an extra layer to help make them memorable. Additionally, by using true stories while explaining concepts we are demonstrating a real-life example of the new learning, thus making it more meaningful for the children.

Talk about past pupils

Jo uses anonymised stories about previous pupils to help the children understand the need to stay safe online and the consequences of sending messages without thinking. Her pupils are always intrigued and shocked to learn that primary school pupils just like themselves have made mistakes, and there are gasps and tuts when they find out what those pupils did wrong. They link future e-safety learning back to these tales about former pupils – and the relatable nature of the stories makes them memorable. Similar anecdotes could be used to reinforce learning in a whole range of lessons in primary schools.

Engage the emotions

Joy and sadness, while being opposite emotions, are equally as powerful when delivering explanations. Using a funny story or making children laugh will make for a memorable experience and the children will link the emotion to their learning. Pupils in our school hunt through fake 'poo' to learn the skill of analysis required to be an archaeologist and observe the result of a banana sandwich going through (and coming out of) a representation of the digestive system! Similarly, stories which allow pupils to empathise with people can help them to understand new concepts more clearly.

Analogies

Analogies can help teachers to explain or clarify a concept. It might be linked to some resources, like the different fruits which can help to demonstrate the comparative sizes of the planets, or it could be something the children are familiar with which is used to feed into an explanation. A workshop group who explained the story of Moses to Year 4 children used a rope to demonstrate how long ago the pharaohs were in power. A child with a recent birthday stood at one end and the increments along the rope showed centuries, millennia and, eventually, the time of the Old Kingdom in Egypt. The children could easily relate to the analogy as they were all a similar age to the child and could see how far along the rope the Ancient Egyptians had lived.

3. Act It Out

How can drama strategies enhance my pupils' understanding?

This strategy goes beyond the relatable connections in the previous one. In acting out, the children get to physically do or be something which helps clarify the new learning for them. Drama techniques are used throughout primary schools, with pupils and teachers dressing up as characters from books or the past and pretending to live or behave as they would. Although getting into role can be a great way to learn about other people, this strategy is about more than dressing up and drama. Pupils and teachers can act out word problems, concepts and processes to deepen children's knowledge or enhance their understanding.

When learning about the rainforest, children in Sam Blaker's Year 3 class encountered sloths and learned about their characteristics. Upon discovering that sloths move in the trees at a rate of three metres each minute, the children marked out the distance and Sam put a one-minute timer on the board. The children had to judge the distance and adjust their speed accordingly. This helped them to appreciate how slow a sloth really is so they could understand why there is often algae growing on their fur.

Similarly, our special educational needs coordinator, Debi Daisley, has used drama in the later years of primary school to explain how particles move in solids, liquids and gases:

In the first science lesson in a series about changing state, I revisited particle theory of solids, liquids and gases using the CPA (concrete, pictorial, abstract) method, in the best way I could think of considering we were talking about atoms! First, using the children as atoms, we acted out being a solid, a liquid and a gas in terms of particle proximity, bonds and vibration/movement. Although this was arguably concrete, it was still a big jump for some children from this to a pictorial representation, so we recreated the three states again using tennis balls for the atoms. In groups, the children had buckets and balls and had to show me the three states, explaining what they were showing. This gave me some feedback about their understanding.

From this we moved on to drawing simple pictorial representations of the three states of matter using small circles to represent atoms. We used peer assessment/feedback in pairs to check the drawings were accurate, and that each child could talk about the proximity, bonds, vibration and movement within each of the states. We then moved on to think about their properties.

In science lessons like the one Debi describes, learning is sometimes so far removed from children's experiences that acting things out is vital to reinforce our explanations. In lessons about electricity in Key Stage 2, children have been used to act out an electrical circuit: certain pupils become the switches, with bean bags being passed around the room to represent the current and how it can or cannot complete the circuit based on the position of the switches. In Key Stage 1, teachers have used the children as parts of an ear to show how we hear sound, with cling film representing the ear drum and some cardboard bones joined with split pins. In Year 2, children have dressed up as bees, with Velcro pads on their heads, to demonstrate pollination. The bees had to go around and pick up pollen (Velcro balls) from flowers (other children) and distribute it to other flowers.

4. Phone a Friend

When is it effective for pupils to explain ideas to each other?

In the first opening scenario, Sofia's problem is that her explanations use vocabulary which is too advanced for her class. Arguably, it would be more useful for a child to stand up and explain the concept. This is sometimes a useful strategy to use in lessons, especially if there are children with a deep understanding who could become the expert.

When questioning her class, and especially when children are chosen to answer at random, Jo allows children to 'phone a friend' if their response is incorrect or they aren't sure. After all, we are fostering an ethos in which it's fine to get things wrong and not know something. Pupils can then pick from others who raise their hand to explain. The child who was originally called upon must then either repeat the answer given by their friend or explain the same concept in a slightly different way.

Teacher: Why have we now got twelve 10s in the 10s column ... Ayyan? (Teacher is holding back the name to ensure attention from everyone before directing the question specifically to Ayyan – see the 'Involve Everyone' strategy in Chapter 6.)

Ayyan: Erm ... I don't know.

Teacher: Phone a friend then.

Ayyan: Okay, Grace – why are there twelve 10s in the 10s column?

Grace: Because we exchanged 100 for ten 10s. We rearranged the number to make it easier to do the calculation.

Teacher: So, Ayyan, why are there twelve 10s there?

Ayyan: Because we needed to rearrange the number to make it easier. We exchanged 100 for the ten extra 10s.

There is an expectation that the original child must first listen to the question so they can repeat it to their friend, and they must also listen to the explanation and try to understand it. Their response to the teacher will reveal whether they have learned from the explanation given by their peer. The teacher can then call on that child later to answer a similar question to check their understanding.

If, as teachers often find, some of the class have already acquired a skill that others still need to learn, pupils can be paired or grouped with a friend who can explain the new concept to them and guide them in their learning. This has been used successfully in Key Stage 2, especially after some quick-fire teacher training for those in the mentor position. We have used this in the teaching of time, a concept which some children understand with ease – those children who practise it daily by responding to their parents or wearing a watch – and with which other children really struggle. By pairing children up and giving them appropriate resources, the more knowledgeable child can mentor their friend in the new learning.

5. Concrete, Pictorial, Abstract (CPA)

How can I solidify pupils' understanding in maths?

Imagine you purchase a new flat-pack wardrobe. You must work out how to put it up. There are three main ways in which you may be given an explanation: (a) the company will provide you with written instructions, (b) there may be diagrams, photos or cartoons of each step or (c) you may receive a visit from an expert (highly unlikely though that is!) who will demonstrate how to do it, letting you try out each step. Which explanation would be the most useful? Which would be the least useful?

In teaching, it is easy to jump directly into the abstract explanation of a new skill, option (a), rather than starting with concrete examples, option (c). Some subject areas are naturally suited to teaching by starting with concrete explanations. In art, you rarely see pupils reading about artists before they look at their artwork. Similarly, PE lessons require the active use of concrete resources in every lesson, occasionally using diagrams or videos to complement any explanations. Teachers can transfer the use of resources in explanation from these subjects to other lessons, particularly maths.

Richard Skemp explains why a 'relational' understanding of mathematics is more effective in the long term for pupils than an 'instrumental' understanding.[3] When children understand something relationally, they can explain why they choose a certain equation or follow particular steps – the relationship between their calculations and the concept. On the other hand, when children understand something instrumentally, they simply know what to do, rather than why. Sayings like 'just add a zero' for multiplying by ten or

---

3   Richard Skemp, Relational Understanding and Instrumental Understanding, *Mathematics Teaching* 77 (1976): 20–26. Available at: https://alearningplace. com.au/wp-content/uploads/2016/01/Skemp-paper1.pdf.

'take the decimal points out and put them back in afterwards' for multiplying decimals promote an instrumental understanding which can feed misconceptions. The CPA strategy solidifies a relational understanding as the children experience multiple representations of mathematical concepts in concrete, pictorial or abstract form. Several studies have supported the use of manipulatives to help children relate the abstract concept to its explanation.[4]

Historically, the use of maths equipment in lessons has been reserved for children with specific needs or those who are struggling. Recent developments within the various Maths Hubs around the country have made a more positive move towards grounding mathematical understanding in concrete representations.[5] Inspired by the maths curriculum in Singapore, teachers are realising the benefits of using concrete manipulatives and pictorial diagrams and cartoons (including the bar model) to deepen pupils' understanding of simple and complex mathematical concepts.[6] The CPA technique means that all children are exposed to explanations with resources, and some lessons require everyone to use the equipment.

Concrete – using manipulatives to demonstrate the concept

Explaining concepts using concrete resources in Key Stage 1 can happen when children sit in the carpet area to gather

---

4 See, for example, Lady Bridget Plowden (chair), *Children and Their Primary Schools. Report of the Central Advisory Council for Education (England)* [Plowden Report] (London: HMSO, 1967); Doreen Drews and Alice Hansen (eds), *Using Resources to Support Mathematical Thinking: Primary and Early Years* (Exeter: Learning Matters, 2007); and Sir Peter Williams, *Independent Review of Mathematics Teaching in Early Years Settings and Primary Schools. Final Report* [Williams Review] (Nottingham: Department for Children, Schools and Families, 2008).

5 See http://www.mathshubs.org.uk.

6 See Liu Yueh Mei and Soo Vei Li, *Mathematical Problem Solving – The Bar Model Method: A Professional Learning Workbook on the Key Problem Solving Strategy Used by Global Top Performer, Singapore* (Singapore: Scholastic Teaching Resources, 2014).

closer to the teacher. Key Stage 2 teachers often sit at one table with the pupils gathered around. Specifying who stands where ensures that those who require help to concentrate are close by. Explaining and demonstrating with the concrete resources is easy and, whether on the carpet or around a table, many children are close enough to join in if required.

As well as seeing the teacher explain and model a concept using concrete resources, it is arguably more important for the children to get the chance to manipulate them too. It is only by them exploring the resources and engaging in high-quality discussion with a partner or an adult that they can deepen their relational understanding.

There are plenty of ways to use concrete examples to aid explanation across the primary maths curriculum:

♦ Make and partition numbers of varying complexities (including decimal numbers) by using base 10 blocks or counters on a place value mat. These can be used to demonstrate the exchanging or regrouping which occurs during some written methods for calculating.

♦ Name and manipulate fractions using different coloured interlocking cubes or counters.

♦ Compare numbers using scales or number balances.

♦ Calculate all four operations mentally using people, objects, (place value) counters or cubes, including grouping and sharing for division, sometimes on a place value grid.

♦ Create arrays using counters, cubes or pin boards for multiplication and division.

♦ Add to 10 using bead strings, interlocking cubes or tens frames.

♦ Use shoes or people to create a bar chart, Venn diagram or Carroll diagram.

Pictorial – using diagrams or pictures to represent the concept

The pictorial part of the strategy moves from showing the maths with resources to representing it on paper. It is the step before the numbers and symbols, but it is sometimes best shown alongside any calculations. A pictorial representation can be as simple as a cartoon which shows what is happening or a diagram of the manipulatives used. Simple addition and subtraction calculations can be represented in a part–part–whole model (as shown below). This is used throughout Key Stage 1, along with other models, to reinforce the children's understanding of the calculations.

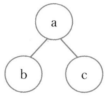

$b + c = a$, $a - b = c$, $a - c = b$

In a similar way, arrays can be used to show multiplication and division pictorially:

$3 \times 4 = 12$, $4 \times 3 = 12$ $12 \div 3 = 4$, $12 \div 4 = 3$

As well as using cartoons and diagrams, the bar model is another powerful tool to promote understanding of many mathematical concepts and word problems in a pictorial way. A bar can represent a whole and can be split according to the skill being learned or the word problem being solved. You can see the four operations represented in the bar model diagrams below, and they are also incredibly useful for showing other areas of maths, including fractions.[7]

Addition and subtraction:
$b + c = a, a - b = c, a - c = b$

a	
b	c

Multiplication, division and fractions:
$a \div 5 = b, b \times 5 = a, a \div b = 5$, ⅕ of $a = b$, ⅗ of $a = b \times 3$

a				
b	b	b	b	b

Abstract – using the correct mathematical symbols and digits to show the concept

Finally, the teacher explains the abstract maths learning which the concrete and pictorial methods have been used to represent. It is important to avoid falling into the trap of using tricks which can lead to an instrumental understanding. Stick to the real explanation and refer back to the concrete and pictorial examples, particularly with children who struggle to grasp concepts in maths.

---

7   The Thinking Blocks (Math Playground) website has lots of tools for modelling mathematical concepts and word problems using the bar model, particularly for Key Stage 2 classes: www.mathplayground.com/thinkingblocks.html.

A gentle release of the concrete and pictorial methods will happen naturally as the children become more confident when faced with abstract maths problems. Even so, the bar method is a powerful tool for everyone, no matter how competent a mathematician they are. Although this strategy is designed to be used in an order – concrete followed by pictorial and abstract – it is sometimes most powerful when all three representations are modelled by a teacher or used by the children simultaneously. In this way, the relationship between the three representations is clear to the children. On pages 56–57 you can see some adaptable examples of how the three methods can be used together.

Helen Drury suggests that the CPA approach should be used alongside the four purposes for mathematical tasks: exploration, clarification, practice and application.[8] By completing activities which satisfy the four purposes using different representations, the children should become more confident, competent and fluent mathematicians.

Although all the examples in this chapter are about maths, concrete and pictorial strategies can be transferred to other curriculum subjects. In English lessons, drama can form the basis of concrete explanations before moving on to diagrams and cartoons to help the children understand the learning. A team of English experts have suggested that making text structures visible in reading lessons helps children to develop a solid comprehension of a text.[9] Pie Corbett recommends using physical movements and text maps before children complete pieces of writing.[10] For more concrete examples from other subjects, including science, see the 'Act It Out' strategy earlier in this chapter.

---

8   Helen Drury, *Mastering Mathematics: Teaching to Transform Achievement* (Oxford: Oxford University Press, 2015).
9   Jane Oakhill, Kate Cain and Carsten Elbro, *Understanding and Teaching Reading Comprehension: A Handbook* (Abingdon: Routledge, 2014).
10 See www.talk4writing.co.uk/about.

Concept	Concrete	Pictorial	Abstract
Calculating using column subtraction	Use cubes or counters on a place value grid to show the regrouping/exchanging taking place.	Draw Dienes blocks or counters and cross out/add in to show regrouping/exchanging.	Calculate using column subtraction.
Finding fractions of an amount	Use manipulatives to divide a whole number into groups (denominator). Choose the correct number of groups (numerator) and add those together to find the fraction of the original number.	Draw one bar which shows the whole and another which is split into parts (denominator). Write out the values of the whole and the parts. Highlight the number of parts (numerator) you need (e.g. to find ¾, highlight 3 out of 4 parts). Add up or multiply the values of those parts.	Write calculations which show the steps taken to find the fraction of an amount. For example, for ¾ of 48: $48 \div 4 = 12$ $12 \times 3 = 36$

Concept	Concrete	Pictorial	Abstract
Equivalent fractions	Use cubes to make some bars which are the same length. Split into parts according to some equivalent fractions.	Draw bars of fractions (or use Thinking Blocks from Math Playground to make bars). Split bars into certain denominators. Find equivalent fractions. Show how each piece has been multiplied or divided to make the new fraction.	Use multiplication and division of fractions to find equivalent fractions.
Multiplication, division, square numbers and square roots	Use cubes or peg boards to make arrays.	Draw arrays using dots or crosses and squared paper.	Write out the calculations using digits and symbols.

6. Just Tell Them

What is the best way of introducing a new concept?

There are some occasions when engaging children's curiosity through questioning about their learning is important. We will cover some strategies for this later in the chapter. Often, it is more valuable to explain to the children first and then use questioning to deepen their understanding, rather than going back and forth through many wrong answers.

Questioning for understanding is a vital ingredient of great teaching: it can provide essential feedback to the teacher about how much the children already know. However, when teaching new skills and knowledge to a class, it is important to reduce the amount of time wasted with answers which aren't based on prior learning. Laura Nichol discovered this during a lesson about the properties of shape in Year 1. She knew that questioning can help children to gain a deeper understanding so she decided to start with a simple question:

Laura (showing the pupils a square): *What is this?*

Child A: A shape.

Laura: Yes, it is a shape. Well done. Now which shape is it?

Child B: A circle.

Laura: A circle is a shape but it's not this one. A circle is round. (She shows them a circle.)

Child C: It's a triangle ...

Many 'good try's and 'nearly's later, she decides that asking the children perhaps wasn't the best place to begin and that her pupils may be picking up misconceptions from each other. When she came to a similar lesson the next year, she started by explaining to the children that the image showed a square. The class segmented and then blended the word 'square', having seen it written down. She also explained to her class that it was a square because it had four sides of equal length. The children searched the room for examples of squares and were able to point them out. Laura was then able to show the children another shape and ask what was the same and what was different about the two shapes, to ensure they had a firm understanding of the properties of the shape. Thus, her explanation started more like this:

Laura (showing the pupils a square): *This is a square. What do we call it?*

Pupils: A square.

Laura: What can you tell me about squares?

Child A: They have four sides.

Child B: And four pointy bits.

Laura: Those pointy bits are called vertices. So what can you tell me about a square?

Child B: It has four vertices.

Rather than spending time going back and forth through many wrong answers, those seconds have been better spent introducing new vocabulary and reinforcing pupils' understanding.

7. Plant Questions

How can I engage children's curiosity through explanations?

We need to open gaps before we close them.

Chip Heath and Dan Heath[11]

Every year, Jo and her class hunt through the books in the reading corner looking at first lines. They discuss what makes a good first line and which book they would most like to continue reading. What is it that makes these openings so effective?

♦ Where's Papa going with that axe? (E. B. White, *Charlotte's Web*)

♦ There is no lake at Camp Green Lake. (Louis Sachar, *Holes*)

♦ I found him in the garage on a Sunday afternoon. (David Almond, *Skellig*)

♦ There was a hand in the darkness, and it held a knife. (Neil Gaiman, *The Graveyard Book*)

♦ Marley was dead, to begin with. (Charles Dickens, *A Christmas Carol*)

♦ Beegu was not supposed to be here. (Alexis Deacon, *Beegu*)

The conclusions drawn are always the same: the best books plant questions in the reader's head, making them want to read on and discover more. The same can be said for teachers' explanations. We need to hook pupils in to the learning to preserve their interest.

The Heath brothers describe this as "the 'gap theory' of curiosity".[12] They describe how trailers for news programmes or

---

11 Heath and Heath, *Made to Stick*, p. 85.
12 Heath and Heath, *Made to Stick*, p. 84.

movies give a small amount of information about the story as a teaser to prompt the audience into asking questions and wanting to discover more. They also explain how making people realise that there are gaps in their understanding can help them to crave the knowledge to fill those gaps. Planting questions and asking for predictions is an effective way of making children curious about the learning to come. We must make the children *want* the knowledge and skills we are planning to teach them, before we actually give an explanation.

In contrast to the previous strategy, 'Just Tell Them', planting questions requires us to hold back information from pupils so they are curious to discover new knowledge. Sue Smith, in her explanation about Germany in 1939, followed her opening sentence with this: "There are two reasons why this is so important to me ..." What are the two reasons? That question was immediately planted into her pupils' minds. She kept them waiting, deciding not to jump straight in to a clarification of that statement. They sat diligently waiting to discover what those two reasons were and, eventually, they did.

Here are some other strategies for planting questions and fostering curiosity about the learning to come.

A mysterious explanation

A very simple but effective way of planting questions is to give children an explanation of something with the main point removed. In this way, they discover clues about a new topic while trying to guess what it actually is. In guessing, they will be finding links to what they already know. For example:

_____ *was probably born in Akhetaten, Egypt in the year 1346 BC. _____ was a king who reigned for around nine years. He was about 18 when he died. The reason that _____ is so*

well-known is because, along with his body, his treasures were
uncovered in 1922 by British archaeologist Howard Carter.

More or fewer clues could be given based on how much you
expect the children to know about the content. This could be
delivered in a variety of ways depending on the age of the
pupils and the aim of the lesson. The discussion which follows such explanations is vital, as are the questions the
children ask each other and you while they try to decipher
the challenge with which they've been presented.

Predict the learning

Another way of planting questions is to introduce the new
concept and ask the children to predict what it is. This is
particularly effective when the new learning involves
technical vocabulary which the children may not have
encountered before. Jo starts some lessons by asking the
children, "What is ...?" – for example, "What is a square
number?" Her pupils then write down their ideas on sticky
notes. Some responses are linked to the clues in the words,
sometimes they are random guesses, sometimes the children
give a partial explanation and very occasionally a pupil
provides a perfect answer. Here are some responses:

Child A: A number written inside a square.

Child B: It's to do with timesing.

Child C: It's a number with no curvy parts, like 4 or 14.

Child D: It's when you times a number by 1 ... or 0 ... or by
itself.

Child E: It's when you make a square and all the numbers
around the outside are added together.

In this way, the children have given the teacher a large
amount of feedback about their understanding. From a

short walk around the classroom, she knows that her pupils are starting from a point of very little knowledge. The children could each place their sticky note in the middle of their table, on the board or keep it private by sticking it in their book. Finally, the teacher says, "We'll return to your predictions at the end of the lesson and see if any of them are correct or close." This announcement feeds curiosity and gives the lesson a purpose, thus engagement is secured.

This scenario would be followed by an explanation of square numbers using peg boards, multiplication grids and arrays. The children could practise making square numbers using any resources available to them, eventually moving on to the abstract calculations and perhaps even discussing square roots. Finally, the teacher must, as promised, refer back to the predictions given by the children. This opens up a discussion about which statements are wrong, which are right, which are partially correct and, most importantly, why this is the case. Thus, the guessed answers to the opening question become a reference point with which the children can compare their new knowledge.

Although this method contradicts the 'Just Tell Them' strategy, it can be useful when the children have just enough knowledge to enable them to make a reasoned prediction. In our example, the children already know what a square is and what a number is; therefore, their prediction will be based on prior knowledge. Later in the lesson, the children will be able to give a sensible reason why they are called square numbers, using their prior knowledge to recognise squares in the arrays they make. On the other hand, if no such links exist in the new learning, then it could be more appropriate to just tell them.

Reflective Questions

- Does my explanation use children's prior knowledge and experience as a hook into the new learning?

- Am I using all possible opportunities to make the explanation clearer – for example, demonstrating with concrete resources, pictorial representations or drama techniques?

- Is my explanation clear and concise, especially when tackling challenging learning?

- Am I using the correct technical terms and avoiding potential misconceptions?

Chapter 3
Modelling

Sarah, the trainee teacher

Sarah was approaching the end of her final teaching place-ment. She was enthusiastic and had built a good rapport with the children. She took on the responsibility of planning a short unit of work on performance poetry and put a great deal of effort into researching, choosing and rehearsing poems to share with the children. She wanted to ensure that she introduced the children to a broad variety and that her delivery of the poems would be impressive. The hours she spent preparing were longer than the lessons themselves! The initial lessons went well – the children showed high levels of engagement, fully appreciating Sarah's performance and enjoying performing poems in small groups. However, when they were asked to write their own poems to perform, their energy levels took a nosedive. Despite being given a list of success criteria, some children barely managed to start and others wrote scarcely concealed copies of the poems they had performed. Sarah felt disappointed with the outcome and reflected on what she could do differently next time.

Jon, the Year 4 maths teacher

Jon introduced his class to finding a percentage of an amount by modelling how to find 10% of a number. He varied the numbers and modelled this several times, explaining that in order to find 10%, you divide the number by 10. He invited a child to come to the whiteboard to find 10% of a number and the child was able to explain confidently the stages he was following. The class completed a question independently and Jon reviewed this with them before asking them to continue working through several examples. As the examples continued, the children were asked to find 50% and 25% of a number. When Jon marked the children's work, he couldn't understand why so many of the children had divided by 50 to find 50% and had divided by 25 to find 25%.

Modelling – What It Is and Why It Matters

Knowing our pupils well is something to which we all aspire, but a frequent cry resonating in many staffrooms begins with, "I assumed they wouldn't ..." or "I assumed they would ..." Consciously, and sometimes unconsciously, we make assumptions that help us to navigate daily life. However, these suppositions can have a profound effect on the way we interact with the children in our class and can impact on their learning. It is worth taking some time to question and challenge our assumptions if we are to be effective in helping children to learn.

Assumption 1: Underestimating them

To encourage all children to aim high, we need to demonstrate that we have high expectations. When children are actively engaged in their learning, they may surprise you with their thinking and problem-solving skills or a piece of written work that exceeds all that has come before.

Assumption 2: Thinking they don't care

If children don't fully engage in lessons, it can be easy to assume that they aren't interested in making progress and haven't yet taken responsibility for their own learning. Fundamentally, most children prefer to succeed in lessons, so what's holding them back? Your classroom environment is supportive – you have developed good levels of trust and mutual respect – so why do some children appear to not be bothered about their learning?

Learning something new can be a stressful process – remember that adults as well as children may feel anxious and confused when presented with a new challenge. If children have a fixed mindset, they may well seem like they don't care. Engaging in work which causes struggle can quickly propel them into panic mode. Why should they keep trying? How will their peers perceive them? They may end up feeling tired, unable to concentrate and upset.

Many teachers wonder why children don't ask for more information or clarification. Dylan Wiliam notes that conversations with pupils reveal that if a pupil does not understand an explanation after having it explained a second time, they will often pretend they have understood it because they don't want to take up any more of the teacher's time or they are worried about appearing foolish.[1]

Assumption 3: Overestimating what they already know

Using responsive teaching – quick, wide-reaching questioning and moving around the classroom frequently, checking progress in books – keeps not only the children on track, but also us and our plans. Don't be a slave to your plan because sometimes you need to loop back and take the time to re-teach key points. Determining what they do and don't already know is never going to be an exact science, but our strong base of knowledge can make us forget the journey we

1 Wiliam, *Embedded Formative Assessment*, p. 135.

took to acquire it, so it is important to stay reactive during lessons. Chip and Dan Heath call this "the curse of knowledge": "Once we know something, we find it hard to imagine what it was like not to know it."[2] They call this a curse because it is difficult to put ourselves in our pupils' shoes; we cannot relive the process that we undertook to gain this knowledge originally.

Teaching can be unpredictable. Dylan Wiliam points out that what pupils learn is not necessarily what teachers intend. It is helpful to remember that we should challenge our assumptions about our pupils' prior knowledge and frames of reference. He stresses that "children are active in the construction of their own knowledge".[3] They are constantly trying to make sense of the world around them, and the result is not always what we anticipate.

For example, Mel has been using peer assessment as a means to involve pupils in the feedback process and to deepen their learning for many years. Even so, it was only recently that she gained an insight into the connections some pupils were making. A Year 6 child entered the classroom after spending ten minutes out of class working on spellings with a teaching assistant. The class were just about to assess each other's work. She asked the child, who was familiar with the process of peer assessment, to "find a peer and sit down", and was surprised by the blank look she received in response. Through discussion, it emerged that although he fully understood the task, he had made a different connection for the word 'peer' – living in a seaside town, he had substituted the definition of 'pier'! Several more children agreed with this as their understanding of the word. Although they would have had the word 'peer' defined by previous teachers, the connection they made was certainly not the one intended – an example of prior knowledge acting as a surprising anchor for new information.

---

2   Heath and Heath, *Made to Stick*, p. 278.
3   Wiliam, *Embedded Formative Assessment*, p. 75.

This leads us to modelling – what it is and why it is important. Modelling is defined as an instructional strategy in which the teacher demonstrates a new concept, process or task and pupils learn by observing it. Research has shown that it is a particularly effective teaching tool as it allows the pupils to observe the teacher's thought processes and encourages them to learn through imitation. According to the social learning theory proposed by Albert Bandura, "Learning would be exceedingly laborious, not to mention hazardous, if people had to rely solely on the effects of their own actions to inform them what to do."[4] He points out that it is fortunate that most human behaviour is learned "observationally through modelling". Observing others tells us how a behaviour or a task should be performed in a far clearer way than listening to a description does.

In the primary setting, you need to show the children what your expectations are from their very first day. Anything and everything you expect them to do is an opportunity for modelling – every behaviour, routine, task and transition. The key to modelling well is enabling your pupils to be able to picture themselves following your lead. Tasks and procedures need to be broken down into step-by-step stages in order to allow your pupils to imitate them. Set a high standard, model that high standard and watch closely as they emulate your model. Pupils then need to be given the opportunity to practise and repeat that practice.

Ron Berger is a wholehearted advocate of sharing models with pupils. He aims for his pupils to "carry around pictures in their head of quality work".[5] He advocates that models of quality work should be admired and should provide inspiration. A model serves to set a high standard and, at the same time, shows the path to attaining that excellence.

---

4   Albert Bandura, *Social Learning Theory* (Oxford: Prentice-Hall, 1977), p. 22.
5   Berger, *An Ethic of Excellence*, p. 83.

Modelling can demonstrate the following:

♦ School community values and how to interact with others.

♦ How to carry out routines and procedures.

♦ The steps necessary to complete a task or process.

♦ Your thought processes – using live modelling.

♦ Pupils as modellers.

♦ Experts as modellers.

There are disadvantages and pitfalls to avoid when modelling. Effective modelling must be highly detailed; each stage must be guided and each transition must be modelled generously. Take our two opening scenarios. Sarah had put a lot of thought and effort into modelling the poetry performance, but left her pupils floundering when the time came to write their own poems. The transition from performing to writing was too abrupt – they would have benefited from having a poem constructed in front of them so they could learn from the process. Jon had overlooked any misconceptions that may arise by only partially modelling how to find a percentage of a number. He did not make it clear that we divide by 10 to find 10% because there are ten lots of 10 in 100, so the pupils did not understand that when finding 25% they shouldn't divide by 25 but by 4, as there are four lots of 25 in 100. A better method would be to introduce 50%, 25% and 20% before moving on to 10%. Teaching in this sequence prevents the possible misconception and deepens the understanding.

There is also a danger in using models too often, particularly in writing. There is a concern that over-modelling can stifle creativity and encourage pupils to engage in producing work that they think will please the teacher. Where is the room for originality? One of the strategies that follows ('Morsels of Excellence') suggests ways to avoid this by sharing more than one model to demonstrate that there is often more than one way to achieve an aim in writing. However, as a starting point, Ron Berger says that he positively encourages his pupils to borrow ideas from models and from each other. Imitation is a great place to begin.[6]

1. Establish the Bedrock

Should I model everything?

Constructive relationships between teachers and pupils are the bedrock of effective teaching. All teachers across a school should have a shared understanding of what they expect in terms of behaviour and the way pupils interact with each other, their teacher and other adults. The expectations should be set high from the day the children begin school. As some children come into Early Years with limited or delayed speech, it is key to model how to speak using a polite tone and Standard English, pronouncing words correctly. If a child asks "Me go wee?" model the correct way of asking, ask the child to repeat this and then reinforce, "Of course you can go to the toilet." It will require perseverance and repetition until it becomes embedded.

Role play with a teaching assistant is also an effective way to demonstrate interaction and how we value and respect each other. For example, in order for the teacher to demonstrate

---

6 Berger, *An Ethic of Excellence*, p. 85.

that she expects every child in the class to track the person who is talking, she may involve the teaching assistant, Mrs Cairns: "Mrs Cairns, when you are talking to me, do you like me to look at you?" In this way, the children are given a model for social interaction and behaviour.

Role play with puppets is also a great way to demonstrate desired behaviours – for example, to encourage children to solve problems using the correct language. Puppets can be shown speaking rudely and hurting each other. Their behaviour can then be analysed and discussed by breaking it down into parts. The role play with puppets is then repeated, this time demonstrating appropriate ways to speak and behave.

At Vale School, we have adopted the acronym HEART to show the values that underpin our school community: Honesty, Excellence, Appreciation, Respect and Teamwork. Teachers model and refer to these values frequently. We believe that having a strong set of school values, and demonstrating them among adults, influences the children's behaviour and how they interact with each other. The children see the cooperation between staff, the sharing of responsibilities, the respect for an adult or child who enters the classroom and the attention that is given to anyone speaking to the class. This provides them with a positive model for being part of the school community.

2. Step, Step, Repeat

Can I afford to take the time to model simple procedures?

Echoing the 'Be Precise' strategy in Chapter 1, if clear and effective routines are embedded in the classroom, expectations can be understood easily and considerable time can be saved at the beginning and end of the day and during the transition from one lesson to the next. For routines to be effective, you must know exactly what you want from your pupils. Before teaching a routine, create a picture in your mind of exactly what it will look like when carried out perfectly. Practise it yourself so that you can demonstrate it exactly as you wish it to be performed.

Anything and everything that your pupils do repeatedly can be modelled – whether that is lining up in alphabetical order at the classroom door ready to go to assembly, moving from classroom to classroom in an orderly fashion, handing out and collecting in books at the start and end of a lesson, moving from the carpet to the tables or stacking chairs at the end of the day. When introducing a new routine to the class, act it out – sit at a table and demonstrate it as if you were a pupil. Consider creating a 'sticky' name for your routine to help the pupils remember it – for example, we use '3,2,1, SLAM' throughout the school to remind the children that we expect them to Sit correctly, Listen, Answer questions and use Magnet eyes (look at the person talking).

To model each routine effectively:

♦ Break the routine down into small stages and model each step. Create a detailed visual guide for your pupils.

♦ Keep accompanying instructions brief and make them a habit. Keeping the words you use the same will enable your pupils to become more independent more quickly.

♦ Consider replacing your verbal instructions with numbers and accompany these with visual cues.

♦ Replace the numbers with visual cues only.

♦ Practise against the clock. How quickly can this routine be completed?

For example, you may wish to demonstrate how pupils should move from the tables to the carpet.

♦ Practise beforehand – walk through the routine you would like to establish; it may highlight a detail that you hadn't considered previously.

♦ Introduce the routine with verbal commands:

1 "Stand up, tuck in your chair."

2 "Walk quietly to the carpet."

3 "Sit down, eyes this way."

♦ Explain that "Stand up, tuck in your chair" will be replaced by the number 1, accompanied by showing one finger in the air. Repeat for the other two commands.

♦ When you would like the children to move from the chairs to the carpets, give them the visual cues only.

♦ Time how quickly and efficiently this can be performed.

This can, of course, be used for moving from the carpet to the tables as well as for other routines. In order for this to become an effective routine, it is important to observe the children closely as they carry it out. Have high expectations and if the procedure is not carried out exactly as you would like, stop them, remodel and send them back to repeat it. Academic tasks that are carried out habitually can also benefit from being modelled – for example, how to present your work, how to annotate a text or how to carry out peer assessment.

3. Live Modelling

What are the benefits of creating a piece of work in front of the pupils?

One of the key advantages of modelling live, as opposed to showing the pupils a model created earlier, is the insight they gain into the process of executing whatever it is you are modelling, whether that is a piece of writing, a mathematical method, a sketch, a design and technology process or a new computing skill. Giving the pupils a window on your metacognitive processes – demonstrating your thinking out loud – as you create is an invaluable guide, particularly when modelling a piece of writing.

Demonstrate the struggle

It is important for the pupils to observe the struggle you experience when drafting a piece of writing. Let them see that you consider five different adjectives before choosing one, and explain your choice. Introduce the 'either ... or ...' method of selecting words – trying out each vocabulary choice before making a final decision. Let them see how much time you take drafting each sentence, changing its structure several times, and that once you have drafted a second sentence, you read both of them back to check that they connect and make sense. Proofread spellings, perhaps replace a noun with a pronoun and explain why this aids cohesion and helps the writing to flow.

You may want to think through some ideas in advance, but take care not to over-rehearse as this can make the process appear too slick and efficient. The children need to witness the development – the perhaps chaotic and rather messy process – and how you arrive at the choices you make and decisions you take. Many pupils will want to join in and make choices and give you advice as you model; try to remind them that, in this instance, you would like them to focus on your narration. How does it differ from their own drafting and editing? The pupils will benefit from witnessing that it is a far from easy process.

Build one together

Another approach is to involve the pupils in constructing a piece of writing together. Continue to demonstrate your thought processes but invite the children to offer suggestions. Encourage them to listen to and build on each other's suggestions. Invite other pupils to explain which version they prefer and why. Ask questions to help them develop their skills, such as:

Which adjective fits best here, either ... or ...?

How can we vary the structure of the sentences more?

How can we change the tone and make it more formal/ informal?

How can we build suspense?

Demonstrate how to use support materials such as word banks, dictionaries and knowledge organisers. If using success criteria, refer back to them frequently. Show the pupils how to edit a piece of writing so that it demonstrates the success criteria.

Model multiple times

When introducing a new concept or method in mathematics, you may need to model this several times. Articulate the process, describing the steps you are taking, and repeat with other examples. Try to anticipate any misconceptions and model examples which will give you the opportunity to address these. In a mixed-ability class, the pupils will grasp the new concept or method at different rates, which is where modelling becomes a scaffolding tool. Invite a confident pupil to model on the board – the key is to choose a pupil who will mimic your steps in detail. This sets the expectation that all pupils are capable of following the teacher's model. Then ask the pupils to take it in turns to model an example in their books for each other. At this point, some pupils will feel confident enough to work independently while others can stay with you, perhaps coming together by the board while you repeat the process. To encourage independence, the teacher can model silently, inviting the pupils to narrate the process. Another option is to watch a video demonstration online and ask them to narrate before commencing work independently.

4. Time for Talk

How much time should be given to pupil talk?

Modelling is closely connected with practice. As well as modelling the rich language that pupils should use in their written work, we must provide them with the opportunity to talk – developing, practising and exploring language before committing it to paper. In this way, the pupils are encouraged to make new words their own. Rehearsing orally underpins the ability to read and write fluently. Consider how much time in class is devoted to teacher talk. What is the right balance in time for teacher and pupil talk? Hearing the correct language modelled needs to be followed by time to practise.

In the primary phase, pupils need to be encouraged to make connections between oral language and written language. Our colleagues in Early Years and Key Stage 1 give children plenty of time to discuss their ideas and rehearse a sentence out loud before writing it down. In Year 1, they are encouraged to make a direct link between the oral and the written sentence by counting how many words are in their spoken sentence. They are then able to check that the written sentence contains a matching number of words, read it aloud and check for any words they have omitted.

Doug Lemov refers to the "art of the sentence", whereby pupils are asked to synthesise a complex idea into a single, well-crafted sentence.[7] This sentence can be rehearsed orally, adding layers of detail at a time. For example, allow a pupil to generate an idea and put it into a sentence. Next, work on the opening of the sentence, then focus on giving the verbs in the sentence more impact.

Drama techniques are of particular value in helping pupils to prepare for writing. Some widely used examples are:

♦ **Hot seating.** The pupil on the 'hot seat' is asked questions and answers in role.

♦ **Conscience alley.** A technique to explore feelings relating to a dilemma. One person walks between two lines of pupils as they offer advice and thoughts.

♦ **Thought tracking.** This allows pupils to identify with a character and express thoughts and feelings.

♦ **Spotlight.** The children are given a limited time to showcase an improvised drama piece.

Focused and well-directed drama techniques can help the pupils to make the language their own.

---

7   Lemov, *Teach Like a Champion 2.0*, p. 288.

5. Here's One I Made Earlier

Will they learn as much from a model created in advance?

Creating a model in advance of the lesson can have many benefits for the teacher. It can show you where misconceptions or difficulties may arise and give you time to plan how to help your pupils overcome these. It can allow you to pinpoint which particular stages in the creation of a medieval siege weapon need to be modelled in detail, or which method of preparation in a food technology lesson needs to be demonstrated carefully or allow you to fine-tune a piece of writing to include features that you would like to demonstrate to the class.

The blank page can be very daunting for a pupil. With live modelling, we can spend time demonstrating how to create an atmospheric story opening, for example. However, if this is the part of a story that is modelled most frequently, pupils can become expert at opening a story but then their work can tend to trail off towards the middle or end. A way around this is for the teacher to write half of a story and spend time deconstructing it with the pupils. What makes it powerful? Why? The children are then asked to continue writing from this point – the tone and register of the story has been set in advance and it is less of a 'blank page' start. There is also the opportunity to live model other parts of the story.

Preparing a model in advance is a valuable strategy because it gives you greater control over the process and allows you to anticipate where your pupils may require further support. The focus shifts from the articulation of your thought processes to a joint deconstruction, analysis and evaluation of the work. However, the merits of this need to be balanced with consideration of the issue that the pupils are no longer witnessing the process of the work being created.

6. Morsels of Excellence

How can pupils' work be used as models?

Often, pupils can be inspired more by the work of their peers than by a model created by the teacher. Keeping and sharing examples of excellence by former pupils is a great way to set high expectations and show pupils what they are capable of achieving. It can be particularly beneficial to show the stages that the pupil has progressed through on their journey to excellence. There is great value not only in deconstructing and analysing the model, but also in discussing how the work isn't necessarily excellent in its first draft, but how, by responding to feedback and carefully editing and improving his or her work, the subsequent drafts have been vastly improved.

Sharing more than one model shows the pupils how they can apply their own creativity to a piece of work and that not all outcomes need to mirror the model exactly. Two or three pieces of work can be very different and yet all model excellence, creativity and originality. There is also a place for sharing work that doesn't meet the high standard that you usually show pupils. You can work together to identify what makes this piece of work of a lower standard than another and look for ways to edit and improve it together. Showing work from a pupil in a higher year group can also be effective, particularly if you want to share good work but not necessarily examples of the same task.

Mel keeps examples of former pupils' English books and regularly draws on these to inspire her pupils. One pupil in her class particularly admired Rebecca's work. Before commencing a task, he would sometimes ask to see Rebecca's book, or if an example of hers was shown to the class he would keep referring back to it as he wrote. Ron Berger refers to this as "tribute work".[8] At first, the pupil's work

---

8   Berger, *An Ethic of Excellence*, p. 85.

borrowed heavily from Rebecca's pieces of writing, but as the year progressed, although he continued to refer to her work, he built off of it and developed a unique, individual voice. He beamed with pride when Mel asked if she could keep his English book at the end of the year. She heard him telling a friend: "I think I'm the new Rebecca!"

7. Model Mistakes

Is it effective to model common errors?

Rather than always modelling high-quality examples, there can be advantages to modelling the common errors and misconceptions that the pupils may have and involving them in the metacognitive processes needed to address these. Role play and humour can be particularly useful for this. Take this example of modelling 'bad habits' when responding to peer feedback.

The teacher, in the role of a pupil, presents her work to the class and tells them that she is proud of it. She works with a partner (the teaching assistant) to follow the steps for peer assessment. The teaching assistant articulates her thoughts aloud as she completes the peer assessment process:

1   Read your work aloud to a partner.

2   Partner highlights where you have met the success criteria (shown here in italics) and any areas for growth

(shown here with underlining) and writes a comment at the bottom of the page.

3   Review your partner's comments.

4   Choose at least one sentence to edit and improve.

5   Write the sentence below your work.

Character description of the Loathly Lady

She was the ugliest living thing he had ever set eyes on, a freak, a monster, a truly loathly lady. <u>Her</u> *limp* hair hung from her *bony, pointed* scalp. <u>her</u> mouth gaped open revealing her *horse-like* teeth *while* her nose was covered in *vile* sores and boils. The scarlet dress made her look <u>as pretty as a butterfly</u>. <u>Her</u> gnarled and twisted hands clutched the crooked stick.

Peer comment: Try to vary the way you start sentences. I don't think your simile fits.

The teacher, in the role of a pupil, looks at which sentence to edit and improve, jumps on the easiest task – adding a capital letter to 'her' – sits down and smiles. Coming out of role, she asks the class for their feedback. They think she should work harder!

She looks back at her work and chooses the sentence with the simile. Talking out loud so that the pupils can hear her thought processes, she decides that if the simile doesn't fit, she will delete the sentence. Again, the class aren't satisfied and ask her to persevere. Speaking her thoughts aloud, the teacher looks at the illustration in the book of *Sir Gawain and the Loathly Lady:*

Her dress is pretty. It does remind me of butterflies a bit in the way it's shimmering. But she's not pretty. In fact, there's a real contrast between her dress and her face. Maybe I could use that. Okay, I'll have another go. "Her scarlet dress shimmered like a thousand butterflies, in stark contrast to her ugly, hideous and deformed face."

She then proceeds to squeeze the new sentence in above the existing one and strike the original sentence out. Once again, the class are not satisfied with this and point out that the sentence should be written beneath the work. They are also able to advise that the original sentence should be left so that you can look back and see your progress. This process can then be repeated with other parts of the description.

Emphasising common errors and looking at how to address them through role play can result in much higher quality work, as the children have the opportunity to reflect on their own areas for improvement.

8. Bring in an Expert

When is it appropriate to use other people as models?

A visit from an expert can have an incredible impact on the children. It is good for them to see you sharing their excitement about learning something new. An expert who is passionate about their field or profession can inspire the children to investigate and explore a subject further, often by sharing their personal stories. Year 4 at Vale School learn through a geography theme called 'River Deep, Mountain High'. Tim Gauntlett, a climber who has explored the world, visits to talk about his expeditions and about those of his late brother. The visit evokes awe, curiosity and empathy, and generates great questions from the children. During the same theme, a triathlete visits to speak about how he uses rivers and mountains for leisure activities and this leads the children into producing leaflets advertising outdoor pursuits.

Parents as experts can also expand the children's perspectives and help them to make connections with the world around them. For example, as part of an enterprise week, a parent who had started her own business creating innovative toys came in to talk to the children about start-up projects.

With technology at our fingertips, using video clips as models can be a refreshing alternative, whether that is a poet reciting her own poem, a mathematician modelling a new concept or a historian enthusing about the intricacies of a political plot.

Reflective Questions

♦ Have I challenged my own assumptions about my pupils' knowledge?

♦ Have I considered any misconceptions that may arise and adjusted my modelling accordingly?

♦ Am I showing a variety of models so that I encourage creativity?

♦ Are my transitions from modelling to independent practice fluid?

♦ At what point should I be encouraging more independence?

Chapter 4

Practice

Anthony, the Year 5 pupil

Anthony is just about keeping up with his peers in maths lessons. He mostly understands what is being taught and he works slowly and steadily to demonstrate his understanding. The reason Anthony works slowly is because he is having to use his fingers to complete simple calculations. For column addition, he uses his fingers for 4 + 3, and to discover if 8 is a factor of 26, he counts up in eights, again using his fingers. If he were fluent in single digit calculations his learning in maths would accelerate beyond many of his peers'.

Jonathan, the time-short teacher

Jonathan knows he is a solid teacher. Pupils make great progress in his lessons and he covers all the objectives of the curriculum throughout the year. He knows how to do well in an observation and, were his head teacher to observe him, he would be judged as outstanding. One thing Jonathan wishes he could do more of is recap what the children have learned. He knows this is a valuable activity for ensuring his learners retain new skills and knowledge, but he is desperately short of one thing to make this happen – time.

Practice – What It Is and Why It Matters

Many primary classrooms are filled with motivational quotations. Jo only displays one: "Don't practise until you get it right; practise until you can't get it wrong." Although its author is unknown, its sentiment is lived out by many people daily. Helen Housby is a goal shooter for the England netball team. While her team are warming up, preparing their bodies for the physicality of the mid-court positions, she is engaging in practice of her most valuable skill – shooting. Spectators watch her pre-match routine with awe. Housby spends the minutes before the match standing in every position in the semi-circle, moving one step at a time and then taking a shot on goal. She stands in the most likely and least likely positions, and sometimes asks a teammate to provide some defensive distraction or coaching. With every shot, she is getting immediate feedback about her position, aim and lift on the ball. Her years of focused practice have meant that almost all of her shots are successful and scoring goals has become a habit.

Practice is about just that: making something a habit or second nature. In education, the 'something' is often a piece of knowledge or a skill. Lessons in primary schools are designed to allow children to learn something new. On the day of the lesson, the learning may only be embedded in the short-term memory. Regular practice of the new learning ensures it is transferred to the long-term memory for quick recall or use. Practice is the cocoon of learning; it's where the magic happens and it creates beauty in knowledge, skills and understanding.

Psychologist K. Anders Ericsson and his colleagues suggest that there are four ideal conditions for deliberate practice:[1]

♦ Pupils must have the motivation to work hard.

♦ Teachers should take into account pre-existing knowledge.

♦ Pupils should receive immediate informative feedback.

♦ Pupils should be given the time to repeatedly practise.

Alongside the time, organisation and conditions for practice in the classroom, pupils' motivation and effort is paramount. Without an understanding of the purpose and potential outcome, children will be far less inclined to put in the work required to practise, especially if they will struggle in the process. Ultimately, this comes down to the growth mindset. Children's appreciation of the work required to succeed is a vital catalyst for them to fully engage in purposeful practice. While it sounds as if this places responsibility on the pupil, it is the role of the teacher to ensure that the activities are appropriate for their children. Being aware of what pupils already know is vital to keep them working in the struggle zone rather than in the panic or comfort zones (see Chapter 1).

Taking learning from the short-term to the long-term memory requires repetition of the knowledge or skill, little and often. American psychologist John Dunlosky suggests that the most effective way of enhancing pupil achievement is to interleave practice activities rather than mass them together.[2] In recent years, we have redesigned our English and maths curricula to build upon learning in a logical and

---

1   K. Anders Ericsson, Ralf Th. Krampe and Clemens Tesch-Romer, The Role of Deliberate Practice in the Acquisition of Expert Performance, *Psychological Review* 100(3) (1993): 363–406. Available at: http://www.nytimes.com/images/blogs/freakonomics/pdf/DeliberatePractice(PsychologicalReview).pdf.

2   See John Dunlosky, Katherine A. Rawson, Elizabeth J. Marsh, Mitchell J. Nathan and Daniel T. Willingham, Improving Students' Learning with Effective Learning Techniques: Promising Directions from Cognitive and Educational Psychology, *Psychological Science in the Public Interest* 14(1) (2013): 4–58. Available at: http://www.indiana.edu/~pcl/rgoldsto/courses/dunloskyimprovinglearning.pdf.

cumulative manner. Practice of previous learning is inter-leaved with new content in various contexts (as shown in the figure below).

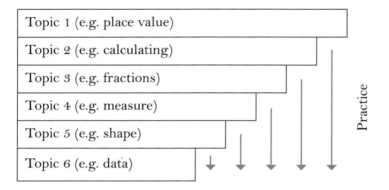

We have found this to be effective in enhancing pupils' knowledge and skills because they are expected to revise, practice and, in some cases, re-learn the previous content across other contexts and in greater depth. The first topic covered each year is the foundation for the future learning and the topics which follow build upon, extend and use the previous objectives within their content. For example, when learning shape objectives in topic 5, the children will be expected to practise the strategies learned in topic 2 (calcu-lating), they will use some knowledge from topic 3 (fractions), area and perimeter questions will require them to practise their knowledge from topic 4 (measure), and throughout all of this they will be revising their understanding of place value (topic 1).

In English, the objectives have been organised in a similar way, with basic skills and knowledge being taught in the first term. Mitchell Hudson, who runs the website Grammarsaurus, calls this the "place value of punctuation and grammar".[3] He suggests that children should learn about the structure of sentences (subject + verb) prior to

---

3   See http://grammarsaurus.co.uk/.

learning about other word classes and the more challenging objectives. Similarly, we focus on the more basic reading skills (decoding and retrieval) earlier, so that pupils can recap them when learning how to interpret or comment on an author's choice of vocabulary. Within a curriculum following these ideas, the children revisit the earlier and most important skills regularly throughout the year; their practice is well spaced and occurs in changing contexts.

The purpose of practice is to facilitate the steady transfer of responsibility for learning. The principles in this book follow the idea that teachers should explain and model new learning before passing the baton to their pupils. We have heard this condensed to the steps of 'I do, we do, you do', with the latter part being children independently practising the learning. Inspired by Erick Herrmann[4] and Doug Lemov,[5] on page 90, in our transfer of responsibility table, we suggest some additional steps on the path to independence. The first two steps are covered in Chapter 3 on modelling, but the latter steps represent a move towards shared practice and independent practice; both of which, if spaced and repeated, can lead to long-term retention and habit building.

English expert Pie Corbett has produced a series of books called 'Jumpstart', which guides teachers in facilitating the practice of vital skills. He states that "children need to revisit what has been taught on many occasions before they grasp or remember an idea".[6] The activities he has devised are designed to take a short amount of time and to remind children of their previous learning. We use these exercises during short interludes at the start or end of a lesson, before the children complete a longer piece of work or while lining up or waiting for an event. Some suggestions require no equipment; others just need mini whiteboards and pens.

---

4   See Erick Herrmann, The Importance of Guided Practice in the Classroom, *MultiBriefs* (12 February 2014). Available at: http://exclusive.multibriefs.com/content/the-importance-of-guided-practice-in-the-classroom/education.

5   See Lemov, *Teach Like a Champion 2.0*.

6   Pie Corbett, *Jumpstart Literacy: Games and Activities for Ages 7–14* (Abingdon: Routledge, 2004), p. vi.

Transfer of responsibility

I do	We do		You do
	I do; you help	**You do; I help**	**You do independently**
The teacher demonstrates the learning.	The teacher works with guidance from pupils.	Pupils work with guidance from the teacher.	Pupils work on their own.
			Pupils work in pairs or small groups.

Times tables practice

EYFS	Counting up and down in multiples.
Key Stage 1	Learning multiplication facts for certain tables.
Lower Key Stage 2	Learning multiplication and division facts for all tables. Tested with four to five minutes to complete forty questions.
Upper Key Stage 2	Learning multiplication and division facts for all tables and also related facts (e.g. $3 \times 4 = 12$, $0.3 \times 4 = 1.2$). Tested with two to three minutes to complete forty questions; the speed of recall becomes the focus.

These short bursts of practice are effective at embedding learning because they are set up as games or challenges which engage the children and require them to recall previous learning and think hard.

The key to effective practice is repetition, repetition, repetition. However, according to teacher and blogger David Rogers, deliberate practice is not simply doing more and more of the same. It's about raising the bar each time.[7] Therefore, when children in our school are practising their times tables facts, their level of challenge increases as they become more fluent. Also, the contexts in which children are using this knowledge become increasingly challenging throughout the key stages (as shown in the times tables practice table on page 90).

Throughout these steps, practice is interwoven with explanation and challenge to ensure a deeper understanding, eradicate misconceptions and promote long-term fluency. When plaited together, these three principles help to move the children from a place of dependence to independence and, finally, to subconscious habit when using their knowledge and skills. Of course, questioning, feedback and modelling also have a part to play in teachers guiding and supporting children in practice.

Challenge

Explanation   Practice

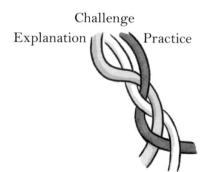

---

7   David Rogers, Fall Down Seven, Rise Eight. Can Schools Grow Grit? *David Rogers* (27 May 2016). Available at: http://www.davidrogers.blog/?p=31/.

Jo is reminded of the importance of perfect practice whenever she is learning to play a new piece of music on the piano. Simply repeating the tune over and over again will not lead to the best possible improvements. She must play it through, identify where she is stumbling and plan and execute specific practice of those elements – whether that is using just her left hand or working out which fingers to use for which notes. Her piano teacher, Brenda Mendelssohn, reminds her that the muscular memory in her fingers will remember the mistakes and learn those through habit if she isn't careful or meticulous in her practice. As Jo repeats this process over and over, her performance will improve until she is playing the tune flawlessly every time – it has become a habit. Only then can she focus on adding in dynamics, adjusting the tempo and ensuring each performance has the required finesse.

When he became the performance director of British Cycling, Sir Dave Brailsford used a similar approach with his cyclists, which focused on making marginal gains to improve overall performance: "The whole principle came from the idea that if you broke down everything you could think of that goes into riding a bike, and then improved it by 1%, you will get a significant increase when you put them all together."[8]

When thinking about learning in this way, it is important for teachers to recognise the marginal areas in which pupils can improve. In some cases, the focus for practice will be different for each child. For example, one child may need to practise his formation of the letters a, c, d, g and o to enable him to write more clearly and spell correctly, while another pupil may need to focus on apostrophes for contraction and how to use them correctly. Both of these areas are almost insignificant in the child's writing as a whole, but improving

---

8   Quoted in Matthew Syed, Viewpoint: Should We All Be Looking for Marginal Gains? *BBC News* (15 September 2015). Available at: http://www.bbc.co.uk/news/magazine-34247629.

these and other elements will result in a significant overall increase in quality.

Homework is a form of practice which is often overlooked. Despite John Hattie's extensive research suggesting that homework in primary schools has a positive effect size of 0.15 (very low), he suggests that short tasks which reinforce previous learning have the same effect as hours spent on a project or problem-solving activity.[9] When activities are chosen carefully to help children practise what they have learned previously in school, confidence can be built and further memory platforms created at home. Weekly practice of reading, times table facts and spelling pays dividends when the children come to use those skills in other tasks. The more children engage in practice of these skills, the quicker and more confident they become at demonstrating them accurately in a range of contexts.

In schools, practice comes in many different forms across the curriculum and, like the numerous products which promise to help you lose weight, all of these practice strategies work best when used as part of a healthy diet of exercises in a classroom with an ethos based around growth and excellence.

1. See It, Hear It, Say It, Write It

How can I give children the optimum conditions for writing?

This strategy is inspired by Pie Corbett and his Talk 4 Writing initiative which is based on children practising aloud before they write.[10] If a child can say something, it is likely that she is reasonably capable of writing it. On the

---

9   See John Hattie's interview with Sarah Montague for *The Educators* (25 August 2014). Available at: http://www.bbc.co.uk/programmes/b04dmxwl.

10 See www.talk4writing.co.uk/.

other hand, if a child cannot say it or has not practised saying it, she is unlikely to be as successful when writing her ideas. Pie's philosophy for teaching writing follows three main ideas: imitation, innovation and independent application.

Teachers begin by introducing pupils to high-quality example texts. Children learn elements of these and practise them together. In the innovation stage, pupils alter the original text and practise writing the new version. Finally, pupils apply what they have learned to a new piece of writing. Throughout the stages oral rehearsal is of paramount importance. Pie explains that through this structure, and the teaching strategies which make it successful, children start to naturally read and re-read their work in their heads, editing as they go. Ultimately, pupils should develop an 'inner judge' which can help them to make decisions about the best words and phrases.

In Chapter 3, we saw how the 'Time for Talk' strategy helps teachers to model and guide pupils' oral work. Through practice, this rehearsal becomes subconscious and children purposefully practise their sentences before they write them down. As children move into Key Stage 2, their oral rehearsal time should naturally reduce as they are able to internalise the practice and self-reflect before they write.

Adam Nicholls, a primary teacher and blogger, uses the following technique. He ensures that the children have heard, seen and orally rehearsed the new skills and vocabulary through high-quality examples. Next, he explicitly teaches the detailed grammatical elements to ensure the children understand what they are writing. This is important in order to avoid misconceptions which are easily picked up when simply imitating another text, and it also feeds into the English skills required within the curriculum. Then, before the children write their own text using the new skills, they rehearse what they will write. This happens through sharing and talking in pairs or groups but also through modelling by the teacher. Adam insists that oral work, as well as written work, must be scaffolded by the teacher. Questions can be used to further pupils' thinking and clarify their ideas. Children should be encouraged to repeat their sentence orally until they are happy with it.

2. Brand the Learning

How can consistency aid practice?

Company branding teams help to make a label recognisable and cleverly place logos, jingles or brand names, such that they lodge in consumers' long-term memories. Often, they employ the type of strategies we used in Chapter 2, such as empathy, humour and stories, to make a concept stick, but it is the consistency which can make it memorable in the long term. Teachers can learn from these strategies to do the same for the skills and knowledge that our pupils are required to learn.

Throughout Key Stage 1 and the beginning of Key Stage 2, we use Alan Peat's sentence types to enhance the quality of children's writing.[11] Each sentence type has a memorable name and each year group focuses on certain sentence types. Therefore, as the children move through Key Stages 1 and 2, they build up a cumulative collection which they can utilise when appropriate. An example that the children encounter early on is a 2A sentence. 2A sentences have two adjectives before a first noun and the same repeated for a second noun. Here are some examples from the children:

When I reached the bottom of the dusty, sandy *staircase, I discovered an* enormous, wooden *door.*

---

11 See Alan Peat, *Writing Exciting Sentences* (Biddulph: Creative Educational Press, 2008).

It was a breathtaking, modern *palace with* terracotta, patterned *tiles.*

Soon, I found myself staggering along a frosty, frozen *path towards an* unusual, deserted *building.*

When they are referred to regularly, the names of these sentence types come to the children naturally and they are incredibly quick to spot them in our reading lessons. Year 4 pupils noticed that J. K. Rowling was particularly keen on simile sentences and that she rarely used 2A sentences. Children soon start to identify these sentences in each other's writing and recognise when a particular sentence type would be effective in their writing. As they move further through Key Stage 2, the pupils have a wealth of sentence types to draw upon, while also being given the freedom to recognise that, at times, a simple, unadorned noun can be more effective. In order to break the rules and be original, you need to learn to follow them first.

Alan Peat has also designed a story structure which can be used in primary schools to help children develop their understanding of plot: Who? Where? Where next? Things that go wrong. Who helps? Where last? Feelings.[12] Once the children understand that most plots can be summarised in this way, they begin to realise how authors manipulate the order, and more confident writers can start to emulate this in their own writing. The consistent use and catchy branding of the plot structure helps it to stick in the children's minds.

Other areas where we have ensured consistency in order to aid memory include:

♦ Mnemonics to help spelling practice and retention of some topic knowledge.

♦ Using famous tunes to practise counting and times tables.

---

12 See www.alanpeat.com/resources/storywriting.html.

♦ Call and response sayings to get the children's attention.

♦ Sayings which reinforce the formation of letters for handwriting or the sounds in phonics.

♦ Technical language used in maths and English lessons.

3. Go Online

What role can websites play in practice?

With the rise in the use of handheld technology, in and out of classrooms, educational websites are increasingly useful for encouraging and facilitating the practice of key skills. Pupils are given immediate feedback on their performance and some sites show corrections to mistakes. There is no marking required, but if pupils have the capacity to log in to a site, teachers can check a child's learning or download whole-class skills reports. We find that the websites that are most successful are those which employ motivational tactics in the form of coins, leader boards, avatars and other rewards.

Recall of times tables and number complements and bonds is vital to learning in maths, and it is something that Anthony, the pupil in the opening scenario – and many pupils in our school – has been missing. We have found that by championing the use of websites in school, the children are more inclined to use them at home. In fact, many children do more online practice outside of school than in.

There is a plethora of websites available for children to use for practice. Some are free, others require a small fee per school or pupil and a few ask schools to part with large sums of cash for access. We have found the best way to check if a site is worth the money is to activate a free trial or request one. It is then quick to see if the children will use it appropriately.

The following table details the sites that are our most used for practice activities.

Site	Subject(s)	Price	Information
BBC Learning	All	Free	Lots of Flash-based games for children. No login required.
Kahoot!	All	Free	The teacher makes or finds a quiz. All children log in at the same time and complete the multiple-choice quiz. Results are downloadable at the end.
Memrise	Word-based – spelling, languages, new vocabulary	Free	Children have their own login. Teacher finds or creates a vocabulary list. Pupils match, type, hear and read words and definitions. Children work at their own pace and Memrise tracks their progress. Tablet apps available.
Sumdog	Maths	Free Premium: small fee per class	Children have their own login. Sumdog completes a baseline assessment for each child and then uses a formula to help them practise to make progress at their own pace. With a premium subscription teachers can specify skills, create assessments and view data for pupils. Tablet apps available.

Site	Subject(s)	Price	Information
Times Table Rockstars	Maths – times tables	Small fee per school Free 30 day trial	Children have their own login. It tests them on multiplication and division facts. These can be set by the teacher for the whole class or small groups within a class. Tablet apps available with a bolt-on.
Times Tables. me.uk	Maths – times tables	Free	Children choose options to help them practise specific multiplication and division facts. They can play online against the clock or there is an option to create and download tests.
Topmarks	Mostly maths	Free	Lots of Flash-based games for children. No login required.

4. Change the Context

When is it appropriate to practise the learning out of context?

An indication of deep learning is that the skill or piece of knowledge can be used effectively by the learner in a different context to the one in which it was introduced. For example, a child has not fully learned the meaning of a new word until they can use it in their own context. Some of our classes have a dictionary corner where unusual but effective words are noted down and displayed along with a brief definition. Recently in Year 4, the word 'seize' was added when the class read it in *Harry Potter and the Philosopher's Stone*. They knew it was related to the word 'take' and so one boy wrote 'seizing turns' instead of 'taking turns' in a piece of work. At this point, the child's learning is very superficial: he knows what the word means but he is unable to use it correctly. With further explanation and (luckily) many more uses by J. K. Rowling throughout the book, the child was able to further understand its meaning and, unprompted, wrote the following sentence in an unrelated task about the trenches of the First World War: "In the pouring rain, we seized our weapons, ready to face yet another group of enemy soldiers."

As teachers, we must provide children with the opportunity to practise their learning across a range of contexts. In doing so, we can give further explanation and clarify children's understanding as well as challenging them further. This is why the CPA technique described in Chapter 2 is so successful at ensuring long-term retention. As well as using maths investigations – which are great for helping children to practise using their knowledge in different contexts – when teaching the strategies for the four operations, we ensure that the children learn to calculate using various units of measure, including time.

Changing the context before the main learning can also help pupils to rehearse certain skills before they are required to use them. For example, during outdoor games sessions, the children may play short handball and netball matches to refine their skills during a unit about basketball. Similarly, we use short activities, called RICs (Retrieve, Interpret, Choice), to help children practise their reading skills:[13]

♦ **Retrieve.** What colour is ...? How many ...? What is the name of the author/illustrator/company/product?

♦ **Interpret.** How is he/she feeling? What might he/she do next? What is the message? How can you tell ...?

♦ **Choice.** Why did the creator choose this music? Why did the illustrator choose these colours? Why didn't they tell us ...?

Many children struggle with interpreting texts and commenting on an author's choice of language or structure. These activities help the children to repeat the skills of retrieval, interpretation and commenting on choices with stimuli that aren't necessarily text based – for example, an advert, image or book cover.

Using a media-based stimulus rather than a text-based one means the children can focus on the thought processes required for the skill, rather than the decoding of texts. As they become more confident in answering these questions orally, and with written responses throughout Key Stages 1 and 2, the children are able to transfer the skills required to the questions asked of them about longer and more complex texts.

---

13 See http://www.mrspteach.com/2015/08/ric-reading-lesson-starters.html.

5. Plug In

How can the first few minutes of a lesson be used for practice?

If, like Jonathan in the second opening scenario, you struggle to find the time for practice, using a short activity prior to a lesson can benefit you and your pupils twofold. Not only are they getting to practise important concepts, but they are also reminded of previous learning so are in a better position to plug into the new learning. Doug Lemov calls a learning warm-up a 'do now' and explains that these should be activities which the children can complete without any input from the teacher.[14] Often these are displayed on a screen so are also known as 'whiteboard workouts'. You can use a simple set of questions (such as a quiz) to help the children plug into the lesson (we explore this later in the strategy called 'Quizzing') but what follows are some other activities which can be adapted to different subjects and year groups.

Practice grid

Our former deputy head teacher, Sue Smith, taught maths in Year 6 for many years and would display a four-part grid at the start of each session. The children plugged into the new lesson by practising skills and knowledge they had previously learned. The grid was based on the ongoing feedback she was getting about her pupils' learning and teachers could adapt it for use across the whole school. Sometimes she would colour code the questions to help the children recognise which area of maths they were practising. The following grid is based on common questions which could be asked in Key Stage 1 classes, along with some possible variations.

14 Lemov, *Teach Like a Champion 2.0*, p. 161.

Which two numbers are odd?	Calculate
12, 15, 18, 19, 22 Variations: even, greater than, less than, multiples of, factors of, divisible by, prime	$18 + 12 = \boxed{}$ Variations: any operation, move the = sign, move the box, use decimals or fractions, make it a balanced calculation
What is this shape called? Variations: more complex shapes (including 3D), their properties, size of angles, lengths of sides	**Fill in the missing numbers in this sequence** **14, __, 18, __, 22** Variations: larger numbers, decimals, fractions with the same or different denominators, time periods expressed in different formats

Concept cartoon

This is a discussion-based activity which can aid the revision of prior learning or preparation for the coming lesson. The children are presented with a cartoon which shows people discussing a scientific or mathematical concept. The pupils must state which person they agree with in the cartoon and give their reasons. Before introducing this as a plug-in activity, it would be helpful if the discussion has been modelled in class so the expectations around language and behaviour are clear from the start. This example comes from Year 2 and is based around plants and seeds in science.

Child 1: You can't put them in upside down – they will grow into the ground.

Child 2: It doesn't matter which way up you plant the seed, it will still grow up towards the sun.

Child 3: On some seeds it matters which way up you plant them but on these seeds it doesn't.

Going APE

APE (Answer it, Prove it, Explain it) can be used across the curriculum but it is particularly effective when used to practise and assess reasoning in maths. This can be done orally (in pairs and groups) or the children could write down their response. These activities help the children to practise fluency in a skill they've already learned while also requiring them to think hard.

Fatima says, "33 is a prime number." Is Fatima right? Go APE!

True or false: 30 × 20 = 6 × 100? Go APE!

What went wrong?

Adam Nicholls likes to put a piece of writing with errors in it up on the board. As his pupils trickle into the classroom, they plug into the lesson by finding where the mistakes are and suggesting what the writer needs to know to correct them. This can be tailored so that it includes some things which the children are finding difficult, revises prior learning or dispels any misconceptions from the previous lesson. The same strategy can be used in maths, particularly with calculations which have been completed incorrectly – the children must find the error. In some classes, a soft toy mascot 'completes' the calculations incorrectly and the children must explain how the maths should be corrected.

Odd one out

Odd one out activities are used in all year groups to inspire pupils to plug in before lessons. Simply show the children a collection of images, words, phrases or numbers and ask them to find the odd one out and explain why they've made that choice. The beauty of such activities is that there is rarely a right answer and the children delve into the depths of their memories to pull on prior learning in their justification. An example is a light bulb, a fire and a bolt of lightning. The pupils must employ their knowledge, from science lessons and of the world around them, to make a decision and explain it.

6. Quizzing

How can more tests be good for pupils and teachers?

An important ingredient in education is teaching children knowledge so they can recall it and use it. Quizzes are ideal for ensuring retention and revision of learning because they are quick to deliver, easy to mark and proven to aid memory. A team of researchers has found that "a spaced-testing (quizzing) procedure along with feedback enhances knowledge".[15] Their findings reveal that quizzing can ensure learning is deeper than just remembering an answer to a particular question; it helps children to link their learning to more complex questions in different contexts.

The key to successful quizzing in primary schools is making the results low stakes. This isn't about ranking children or scoring them. The quizzes we use regularly are designed to remind children of previous learning, check how much they've remembered and help them understand any errors they make. Some quizzes are designed to test a specific area of a subject (e.g. electricity in science); others are more general revision of prior learning and contain questions about knowledge learned in the previous lesson, week, month, term or year.

We arrange quizzes in three different formats in our school. The first two methods can be delivered by a teacher with a small group or a whole class. Sometimes, it is appropriate for pupils to quiz each other; we have found this to be particularly effective when practising times tables facts and spellings. The final format is for the pupils to use quizzes to practise independently.

Class quizzes (for teachers)

This doesn't mean that we take the quiz, although we have done that in our staff meetings to keep teachers on their toes! Instead, it means that the purpose of the quiz is to inform teachers about how their classes are progressing and to help them plan further lessons with an appropriate level

---

15 Mark A. McDaniel, Ruthann C. Thomas, Pooja K. Agarwal, Kathleen B. McDermott and Henry L. Roediger, Quizzing in Middle-School Science: Successful Transfer Performance on School Exams, *Applied Cognitive Psychology* 27 (2013): 360–372. Available at: http://www.academia. edu/2417836/Quizzing_in_Middle-School_Science_Successful_Transfer_ Performance_on_Classroom_Exams.

of challenge. Michael Tidd advocates the use of this type of quiz to review learning:

My aim is never to catch students out, or to reward or punish outcomes. Rather, these assessments allow me to make frequent judgements about how effective my teaching has been, and to adapt it accordingly. It isn't about scores, or percentages, or league tables; it's about tailored assessment to match my students and my curriculum.[16]

Class quizzes (for pupils)

This activity is focused on reminding the children of skills and knowledge learned previously and therefore takes a little more time to deliver. We try to arrange quizzes so the children can mark their own or their partner's work and can receive immediate feedback and input regarding their mistakes. Occasionally, this reveals significant misconceptions or widespread mistakes which must be explained and corrected immediately. We have found it especially important to reserve time for such quizzes.

Self-quizzing

For many years, strategies similar to 'look, cover, write, check, correct' have been used to help children when learning spellings – we remember doing this when we were at school. However, spellings aren't the only thing that can be learned in this way. Inspired by the blogs of secondary teachers at Michaela Community School, we have been encouraging children to practise word definitions, times tables, and historical and geographical facts in this way.

16 Michael Tidd, Why More Tests Are a Good Thing, *Teach Primary* (n.d.). Available at: http://www.teachprimary.com/learning_resources/view/why-more-tests-are-a-good-thing.

Reflective Questions

◆ After an explanation of a new concept, do I give enough class time for the children to engage in practice activities?

◆ Do the practice activities I plan encourage the children to think hard?

◆ Are scaffolds and supports used to aid the children's practice, and are these removed in a timely way to allow them to build independence?

◆ How do I treat mistakes in my classroom? Are they a key aspect of learning and do they lead to intervention when necessary?

Chapter 5
Feedback

Holly, the struggling speller

Now in Year 6, Holly has always been a wonderful author. She reads widely and loves learning new words and phrases to use herself. Her sentences flow with ease and she utilises a variety of structures to keep her reader entertained. Unfortunately, no one has noticed that Holly's writing is improving despite the feedback she receives, not because of it. For years now, since she could read, constructive comments on her written work have focused on only one element of her writing – the spelling. Her work is full of corrections written by her teachers and they always remind her to focus on her spelling. Holly knows she struggles to spell and works hard to write words correctly. If only her teachers would target their feedback at other elements to further improve her writing.

James, the Year 3 teacher

No. The word James uses regularly when asked out for social occasions on a school night. No. Why? It's that large pile of work that needs marking. He understands the importance of written feedback and aims to mark every book before it is returned to the child. This is difficult because his school policy requires two stars and a wish on each piece of writing, a challenge question after every maths activity and both positives and areas for development in non-core subjects. Every day he teaches more lessons – sometimes up to five different subjects – and that means a mountain of marking for him. The root of James' problem lies not in his attitude to assessment but in his school's focus on the quantity of marking, instead of quality feedback strategies.

Feedback – What It Is and Why It Matters

Jo's former head teacher, Bruce Waelend, refers to teaching without feedback as being like a golfer hitting golf balls in the dark. With no light or view of the path the golf balls are taking, the player is simply hitting the shots over and over. Each ball is a new start and a chance to swing better than the previous shot, but the lack of visibility means there is no indication of how the technique could be improved. The moment the sun is up, the golfer can see the extent of their success and adjust their stance, swing or angle accordingly.

Feedback is essential if improvement is going to take place; it allows someone to progress from A to B. It could be a physical journey – using a map, street signs and other directions – or a point along a learning process. Having bought a new piece of technology, users go from a point of not knowing how it works or how best to use it to being confident in making the most of it through a series of steps. They might test a few buttons, try out some operations and instantly know something has gone wrong, causing them to retrace their steps. The device may display error messages encouraging the user to consult the handbook or an Internet forum. Also, some help may come in the form of a friend who already has the device and knows how to use it – an expert.

Each of these interactions – with the device, the handbook and a friend – is a form of feedback.

As the device is used more and more, less feedback is required to use it until eventually it becomes second nature. Think about your phone or TV – how you learned to use it and how easy it is for you to use now. Subconscious feedback helped you get to this point. Nowadays, when you need to use a new feature or app, further feedback – in the form of instructions, error messages, friends or a quick Google search – enables you to become confident. Similarly, in the classroom, children are given new knowledge and skills to aim for. As teachers, we need to help them on their journey: keeping them on track through precise and timely feedback, celebrating their effort to succeed and pointing them towards their next challenge.

The value of feedback in schools is evidenced throughout academic research. The Education Endowment Foundation's Teaching and Learning Toolkit is based on many analyses of strategies common in schools around the world.[1] Feedback is categorised as the most effective strategy (from among those analysed) for improving learning in the classroom; it can have "very high effects on learning" when implemented correctly.[2] In 2015, John Hattie ranked nearly 200 strategies used in the classroom and, again, feedback was among the most powerful.[3] Maria Elawar and Lyn Corno's extensive study discovered that, as well as improving outcomes for pupils, effective feedback can enhance children's attitudes towards subjects and close the gender attainment gap.[4]

---

1 See https://educationendowmentfoundation.org.uk/resources/
   teaching-learning-toolkit.
2 See https://educationendowmentfoundation.org.uk/resources/
   teaching-learning-toolkit/feedback.
3 See http://visible-learning.org/hattie-ranking-influences-effect-sizes-
   learning-achievement/.
4 Maria C. Elawar and Lyn Corno, A Factorial Experiment on Teachers'
   Written Feedback on Student Homework, *Journal of Educational Psychology*
   77(2) (1985): 162–173.

In the golf analogy at the start of this chapter, the golfer is both the teacher and the pupil. How can a teacher adjust and refine their practice if they don't know the extent to which it is making a difference to their class? Likewise, how can a pupil continue to improve their knowledge and skills without precise suggestions about what and how to improve? It goes without saying, then, that feedback is a two-way process:

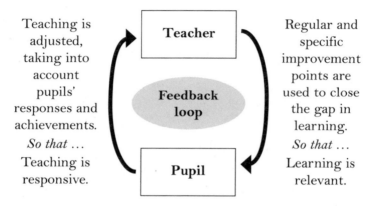

Teaching is adjusted, taking into account pupils' responses and achievements. *So that ...* Teaching is responsive.

Teacher

Feedback loop

Pupil

Regular and specific improvement points are used to close the gap in learning. *So that ...* Learning is relevant.

Some lessons will consist of a teacher setting a task from which they will gain feedback about children's achievement – for example, work based around a brand new topic or skill. Other lessons will consist of the teacher providing feedback to pupils during a task or after a piece of work has been completed. Most lessons will consist of questions, tasks and activities which provide feedback for the teacher and the pupil.

The purpose of feedback, therefore, is to enable teachers to identify the learning gap and address it. Feedback can come in many forms and from many sources: it can be written or verbal, it can come from an adult or a child, it can be self-generated or come from a computer program. The overarching aim is to close the learning gap, thus supporting the child to make progress and to take another step along the journey.

We believe there are four key principles which ensure that feedback is effective for teachers and pupils:

1   Feedback must be useful to the pupil, teacher or, preferably, both.

2   Having analysed an extensive amount of research, the Education Endowment Foundation states that feedback must be specific, accurate and clear.

3   Feedback is most effective when it is immediate and verbal.

4   The time taken for teachers to complete any written feedback must be appropriately balanced with the impact it will have on children's learning. We call this the time versus impact ratio.

When giving feedback to pupils, it is important that we motivate and inspire them to continue to work hard and learn. Dweck suggests that we praise the process children have been through rather than the overall outcome: "'Effort' or 'process' praise (praise for engagement, perseverance, strategies, improvement, and the like) fosters hardy motivation. It tells students what they've done to be successful and what they need to do to be successful again in the future."[5] The Education Endowment Foundation concurs that specific praise is beneficial, especially when it is focused on children's prior learning or targets.

For a teacher's feedback to be most effective they need to consider the bigger picture for their class. Holly, the child in the first scenario at the start of this chapter, is receiving verbal and written feedback which will help her to make some progress. However, spelling will only get her so far in her quest to become the best writer she can be. Teachers need to be acutely aware of the feedback they are giving children and ensure it is focused on specific skills throughout the school year.

---

5   Carol S. Dweck, The Perils and Promises of Praise, *Educational Leadership* 65(2) (2007): 34–39. Available at: http://maryschmidt.pbworks.com/f/Perils+of+Praise-Dweck.pdf.

The following strategies are used across our school to ensure feedback is constructive and efficient.

1. Planning for Feedback

Why should lesson feedback start before the lesson itself?

When planning, we should always consider the feedback children will receive during and/or after the lesson and the format it will take. It is useful to ask the following questions when planning:

♦ How should feedback be organised?

♦ What do I need to know about the children's learning? What do the children need to know about their learning?

♦ Will feedback be written or verbal?

♦ When will the children be given the chance to read, respond to and reflect on feedback?

♦ How will I know which children are doing well? How will they know?

♦ How will I ensure it makes a difference?

♦ How can I adjust the feedback for any specific needs in the class?

These questions help to ensure that the modelling and explanation for the lesson is appropriate, as are any activities used to practise skills. Often, plans will be altered slightly as a result of these questions to ensure feedback is used to close the gap. This doesn't necessarily need to be recorded any-where but it is vital in ensuring that children gain high-quality feedback.

For example, when our Year 4 classes were learning to reflect shapes across a line of symmetry, the plans required the teachers to model this skill a few times on different backgrounds and with shapes at different orientations before the children set about doing the same. This sounded like a fairly well-planned lesson, but in previous years the pupils had really struggled to complete the activities accurately. The Year 4 team adjusted the plans so that as well as modelling how to complete the skill, they also showed the children how their work would be checked – corner-by-corner against the line of symmetry. Some shapes were displayed which were reflected correctly as were others which had been completed incorrectly. As usual in shape lessons, some children could immediately identify the errors whereas others could not. Using mirrors and lines, the teachers demonstrated which were right and which were wrong. This helped the children, particularly those with poor spatial awareness, to see how to check their own work and enabled them to be more successful than if the original plan had been followed.

2. Feedback for Planning

How can I ensure that the feedback I receive feeds forward into my plans?

Teachers receive quality feedback in many ways but the most common are through looking at the work completed in a lesson or having discussions with pupils about the learning. Transforming this feedback into a plan for the next lesson is paramount for creating appropriate learning objectives and ensuring the pupils are making rapid progress. This planning process can start as soon as you begin to gauge pupils' understanding through questioning or as you circulate in the classroom checking work once they are settled. All of these interactions with pupils and their work lead to points for teachers to remember and use. Contrary to popular belief, teachers aren't superheroes; we simply can't remember everything. Therefore, we need some strategies for collating and storing this information.

You may find the following strategies helpful in organising the following day's lessons, without requiring lots of written markings in books or on plans.

♦ **Coloured bookmarks (Key Stage 1).** By using two coloured bookmarks, pupils and staff (including support staff) can identify how successful pupils were in a previous lesson. Support and reinforcement can then be provided to pupils according to their understanding in the form of further explanation, modelling, practice in small groups or one-to-one intervention.

♦ **Coloured dots (Key Stage 2).** Coloured dots are put at the end of a child's piece of work (which they have marked for themselves: right or wrong) to indicate their activity for the next day. A brief explanation of the meaning of each coloured dot is required at the start of the next lesson. The onus is then on the children to organise themselves; the teacher doesn't have to remember each child and what their next step should be.

♦ **Piling.** When checking children's work, simply organise the books into piles based on what the children need to work on. Plans can then focus on explanations of those skills along with some activities to help the children practise them. Planning like this takes time to refine but it is very effective both in terms of its impact and use of time. It requires no written marking and is instead focused on closing the gaps in pupils' learning.

3. Checking versus Marking

How can I assess children's understanding without marking their work?

We all know that marking a set of books takes a long time; rarely does it take less than half an hour. Checking books, on the other hand, can take as little as five minutes per class, so it is a quicker way of achieving the same goal: teachers knowing what children can and can't do and what they need to learn next. Therefore, the strategies mentioned in this chapter follow the belief that checking children's work is more important than putting written markings on it.

Michael Tidd argues that "in the first few moments of looking at a piece of work, a good teacher can take in a fantastic amount of knowledge and understanding about how a child has understood a given taught concept".[6] He explains that a few more seconds spent reading or reviewing the work can give a deeper insight into a child's understanding. Once a teacher has completed that short but valuable check of a child's work, it is up to them to decide whether some written marking will have any impact or whether making a quick note of a misconception or error will suffice.

Therefore, we are increasingly checking – rather than marking – children's work. Of course, pupils are keen to know that their work has been seen by their teacher and it is important that we look at what they have produced in order to appropriately plan what learning must come next. We use a simple tick, stamp or initial to show the children that their work has been checked – an important action for keeping them accountable and expectations high. It is the notes we make, the plans we change and the mini-interventions we

---

6   Michael Tidd, Why We've Got Planning and Marking All Wrong (Part 1), *Ramblings of a Teacher* (5 November 2015). Available at: https://michaelt1979. wordpress.com/2015/11/05/why-weve-got-planning-and-marking-all-wrong-part-1/.

prepare for the next lesson that really make an impact on that child and their learning.

The way in which you make notes, gathered during and after the lesson, can be varied to suit the individual – sticky notes or evaluation space on lesson plans, for example. Rather than laboriously commenting on every child's work, one idea is to start a feedback journal – a book in which notes can be added to store information for future reference and to feed into the learning. Notes can be made about what went well – particularly any pieces of work aiming for excellence, any misconceptions that need to be addressed and any pupils who need support in the next lesson. The information can be gathered in much less time, thereby ensuring that whole-class, group or individual oral feedback to pupils can be timely.

4. Speedy Marking

How I can reduce the time written feedback takes while enhancing its impact?

Like James, the teacher at the start of this chapter, many teachers struggle with the amount of time written marking takes. Along with many other tasks, marking could easily fill a whole working week and more. The key to effective marking is to know when it counts and how to speed it up. The following strategies can help to speed up the process of written feedback.

♦ **Answers.** This is particularly useful for closed maths tasks or grammar activities. On the surface this is very simple: have the answers available in some form so the children can mark their own work. When you dig deeper, it is how the answers are used that can affect the degree of learning taking place. For example, children can mark their own work near the end of a lesson or have access to the answers throughout the lesson, so at any point they can assess if they are on track. They can check their work, complete any corrections and evaluate their progress. They can choose to continue working to become confident, move on to something more challenging or get some help to address their errors. In addition, the children can mark each other's work and spot errors that someone else has made. This means that the teacher can simply check the work and focus on misconceptions and next steps as all corrections will have been made in the lesson.

♦ **Focus your attention.** This is particularly useful in English lessons. In extended written or grammar tasks, asking the children to underline certain elements can help you to quickly check to gauge their understanding. For example, in a lesson about fronted adverbials, a teacher might ask the children to underline the fronted adverbials they have used and circle the commas in their sentences. This not only brings the children's attention to the learning objective, but it also means the teacher can clearly see whether they understand the new concept or not. The same strategy can be used across many subjects to refocus attention on the learning objective.

♦ **Hold a pen.** Make sure that you, your teaching assistant and any other adults are armed with a pen during the lesson. Give the instruction that if they work with a child, they should quickly mark their work to get an idea of how they can help. Also, any further explanation or input can be provided by the adult on the child's work. It is useful if the pen is a different colour to the child's so that any adult help is obvious when checking for a child's understanding. In our experience, children like having their work marked during the lesson as it gives them immediate feedback about their learning and how to take it forward.

♦ **Highlight it.** In all key stages, teachers at our school use highlighter pens to make marking speedy. We use pink to indicate the strengths in children's work and green to show where corrections are needed. Consistent colours and meanings across the school ensure that the children are clear about the feedback on their work and they can focus on the areas highlighted by their teacher (or a fellow pupil). If checklists for success criteria have been used, the colours can be used to indicate whether or not a child has achieved a criterion. Green highlighters are also used to emphasise mistakes which the pupil should correct independently. As pupils move through the school, a green dot can be put close to a mistake (near a calculation in maths or on a line of writing) to indicate where the children need to check, locate and amend their errors.

♦ **Numbered targets.** This strategy is doubly effective when it comes to written feedback: it takes very little time for the teacher to complete and, by its nature, it ensures the pupil reads and understands the comments on his or her work. If there are groups of children in the class with similar next steps, group these targets together and number them. Some teachers may not be happy with a numerical system as it could imply that some targets are more important than others, so different symbols or colours could be used as a code instead. When communicating these targets to the children, teachers only write the number (or other indication) in a child's book. Mostly, this can be done by writing T1 for target one and T2 for target two, but sometimes a target sticker or stamp could be used to focus a child's attention. The onus is then on the pupil to read, understand and write out their target on their work. Targets can be communicated verbally, displayed on the board or relate to a list already stuck in an exercise book.

5. Read, Respond, Reflect (RRR)

How can I ensure my written feedback is making a difference and closing the learning gaps?

At the beginning of this chapter, we stated that one of the key principles of feedback is the relationship between the amount of the teacher's time it takes and the impact on learning for the pupil. Checking books, as described previously, takes a small about of time and is primarily for the benefit of the teacher. Marking books, on the other hand, takes longer and is for the benefit of both teacher and pupil. However, as Victoria Elliot and colleagues at the Education Endowment Foundation observe, "Pupils are unlikely to benefit from marking unless some time is set aside to enable pupils to consider and respond to marking."[7] Consequently, it is essential for teachers to make time for this.

Modelling how you want children to reflect on and respond to your marking will further enhance the impact it can have on learning. This is especially important in September, but it is always worth reminding the children of your expectations for this throughout the school year. Once the children know how to read, respond and reflect, teachers must ensure that this becomes a habit for each piece of work that has been

---

7   Victoria Elliot, Jo-Anne Baird, Therese N. Hopfenbeck, Jenni Ingram, Ian Thompson, Natalie Usher et al., *A Marked Improvement? A Review of the Evidence on Written Marking* (London: Education Endowment Foundation, 2016). Available at: https://educationendowmentfoundation.org.uk/public/files/Publications/EEF_Marking_Review_April_2016.pdf.

marked. Using a different writing implement to ensure there is a physical difference can help the children to focus on the process of editing and improving their work. Pupils know that, when they are using a particular pen, they must be reading, responding to and reflecting on their teacher's marking.

6. Power to the Pupils

How can my pupils help me save time when giving feedback?

Jim Smith, also known as the 'lazy teacher' due to his strategies to reclaim a sensible work–life balance, asks the question: what if teachers worked less and their pupils worked more?[8] With one teacher and up to forty pupils in a class, we simply do not have the time to correct every mistake. James, the teacher in the second opening scenario, is probably trying. An important part of our role in education is to teach and encourage children to become editors, spellcheckers, mistake-spotters and error-correctors.[9]

Simply saying "read it through" or "check for your mistakes" seldom has the desired effect. Instead, we must model the editing and correcting process and guide children through it. Similar to the process described in Chapter 4, we must move through a transfer of responsibility which begins with us modelling the skills required for finding and correcting the errors in our own work. One step along this continuum is the children working together to edit or check and correct work. Eventually, they will be better equipped and more confident when doing the same independently with their own work.

---

8   Jim Smith, *The Lazy Teacher's Handbook: How Your Students Learn More When You Teach Less* (Carmarthen: Independent Thinking Press, 2017), p. 1.
9   See Berger, *An Ethic of Excellence*, p. 97.

As they take the power in giving and getting feedback, there are three important things pupils should know:

1   **What are the expectations?** We can't expect a child who is new to Year 3 to know what a Year 3 piece of art should look like and what makes it successful. A high-quality model should be shared and discussed – pupils should be made aware of what elements they need to include in order to be successful. The expectations should be made crystal clear to the pupils before they give feedback to another pupil or on their own work.

2   **What should I do if I'm giving feedback?** Ron Berger calls this part of a learning journey a 'critique' and, as with other strategies for feedback, it can be oral or written.[10] In primary classes, it is easy for children to get caught in the trap of giving superficial feedback – for example, commenting on presentation. Berger has three rules for giving feedback to a friend and we think these are useful to share with the children and model for them: be kind, be specific and be helpful. As teachers model this critique of their own or a child's work, these principles should be adhered to and mentioned regularly. In a video titled 'Austin's Butterfly', Berger guides children in giving effective feedback about a piece of art a schoolboy has completed.[11] By carefully guiding the pupils with questions and referring to the original expectations, the feedback generated demonstrates how the process can lead to great improvement.

---

10 Berger, *An Ethic of Excellence.*
11 Ron Berger, Austin's Butterfly: Building Excellence in Student Work [video] (2012). Available at: https://vimeo.com/38247060.

3   **What should I do if I'm getting feedback?** It's important to model how to behave when receiving a critique,
either with another adult or child. An ethos of growth
mindset and excellence will provide the foundations for
positive attitudes towards feedback. Children should
expect to work hard to improve a piece of work and they
should respect any suggestions made to them. If the
peer feedback is oral, the children must know that they
can ask questions to their classmate and request help or
suggestions. As with teacher feedback, peer feedback
should not be a one-way process. Again, the 'Austin's
Butterfly' video is ideal for showing children the power
of feedback if it is listened to and acted upon.

7. Project It

How can feedback for one child provide feedback for all?

In recent years, visualisers have become commonplace in
many primary classrooms. As well as being a useful tool for
modelling, they hold an important place in providing timely
and effective feedback during activities. In English and
maths lessons, it is likely to be work in an exercise book
which is projected for all to see, but in more practical sessions, like PE, design and technology or drama, it could be
in the medium of a video or photo. Guided by the teacher,

pupils can discuss the effectiveness of the work displayed and give suggestions for improvements, remembering to be kind, specific and helpful as in peer feedback. While the feedback is given to the one pupil whose work is displayed, the benefits ripple throughout the class as other pupils react to what is said and begin to make comparisons with their own work.

Shirley Clarke, a champion of the use of visualisers for feedback in classrooms, explains its effectiveness as follows: "Evaluation needs to be constant – as the learning is happening – so that changes can be made or new thinking applied *while the work is in progress* rather than retrospectively."[12] She suggests this strategy is most effective when the teacher aims the discussion at where the pupil has best demonstrated the learning, not just where they have completed the task. For example, when a Year 1 child is writing about cold climates and describing the landscape, focus not just on their use of adjectives but their best adjectives and ones they've used beyond any class lists or displays.

8. Post a Comment

How can technology support or enhance feedback?

There is no doubt whatsoever that computers and other devices have transformed the classroom environment and broadened the learning opportunities available to our pupils. Tablets and laptops enable a better ratio of technology to pupils and some schools have aimed for one-to-one device provision. As well as opening up the scope for teaching opportunities, new technology (both hardware and software) has created a plethora of possibilities for feedback.

---

12 Shirley Clarke, *Active Learning Through Formative Assessment* (London: Hodder Education, 2008), p. 134 (original emphasis).

Many apps and websites provide the opportunity for pupils to share their work with teachers and peers, rather than having to attach it to an email. This allows work to be created and edited collaboratively on different devices; we sometimes have thirty-two members of a class editing the same document! Such services are so impressive in their range of features that children in Key Stage 2 are inspired to investigate and use them further outside of school. In this way, any feedback given is accessible to children at all times, whether in the classroom or at home.

Teacher or peer comments

Commenting features within word processors, slideshow editors and spreadsheets allow children and adults to communicate back and forth about a whole piece of work or certain highlighted words and phrases. During or after a lesson, teachers can leave comments on work reflecting overall success and areas for improvement or comments linked to certain words and phrases. Alternatively, after working on their own improvements, pupils can share their work with a certain member of the class. With children checking and commenting on each other's work, all children will receive some feedback which they can use during or after the lesson.

Shared feedback

Simply by using an online document creator, teachers can turn their interactive whiteboards into visualisers. The work can then be read together as a class, commented upon and edited live, and effective peer feedback can be modelled by the teacher. Such services also allow the teacher to effectively 'flick' through the work of the whole class by observing a thumbnail or preview and swiftly moving through all the documents. When her class were using Google Drawings (part of the free Google for Education suite) to create logos for a tourist attraction, Jo spent a minute showing the class each other's previews in her folder in Google Drive. This prompted a brief discussion about the elements which had been included by the creators of the most effective logos. The children were then much more focused on their work in the remainder of the lesson and many more children created successful logos than had done in previous years.

Open up to an audience

As explained in Chapter 1, children produce their best work when they know it is going to be seen far and wide. Why not give your pupils the largest possible audience by publishing it on the worldwide web? The Internet has brought the world into our classrooms but it has also enabled us to display our pupils' work to the world. At our school, we use a writing showcase blog (http://valewriters.blogspot.com) to host a selection of writing from across the school. We encourage staff, children and families to leave comments on the pieces of work. Blogs are free and very simple to set up. Blogger (powered by Google) and WordPress are two of the most popular free hosting websites. One showcase blog prompted a parent serving in Afghanistan to leave a comment on his son's piece of work – something he otherwise wouldn't have seen until his return.

Once the children become familiar with blogs, the possibility that their work could end up in a post is often enough to add motivation and enhance the quality of their work. When Year 4 completed writing based on videos from the Literacy Shed website (www.literacyshed.com), the teachers started by explaining that the best pieces of work would be featured on the showcase blog and that the link would be shared with the creator of the Literacy Shed, Rob Smith. Being huge fans of the website, the children were excited about creating some work which might be shared with Rob and the world. Similarly, when the pupils have written biographies of people who are active on social media, we always send a link to the actual person. Steve Backshall and Bear Grylls are regulars for the 'Adventurers and Explorers' topic. Both are yet to respond, but the fact of the link being sent to them is motivation enough, even for some of the most reluctant writers.

Reflective Questions

♦ Am I using immediate, verbal feedback as often as possible?

♦ Is the feedback the pupils receive kind, specific and helpful?

♦ Are my pupils working harder than I am?

♦ Do I ensure that the children have time to read, respond to and reflect on written feedback?

♦ Are my lessons flexible and based on feedback from the performance of pupils?

♦ Does my feedback foster a growth mindset and encourage the children to aim for excellence?

Chapter 6

Questioning

Amy's learning nerves

Amy was a conscientious pupil who was prepared to work hard and had a keen desire to learn. However, she found herself becoming nervous at the beginning of every lesson. What if she didn't understand? What would her classmates think if she admitted she didn't understand? What if she were asked a question she couldn't answer? She found refuge in saying, "I don't really know", whenever she was asked to share her opinion.

Szymon's permanently raised hand

Szymon measured his success in a lesson by how many times he was asked to answer a question. He liked to participate and enjoyed offering his opinions to the class. He took pride in being the first pupil to put his hand in the air and sometimes felt as if he would burst if he wasn't asked to respond. The relief and delight at being chosen was often short lived as he struggled to frame his contribution to the class discussion. His energy had been focused on being selected rather than on the words and ideas he wanted to share. He often felt dejected

131

when the teacher suggested he took more time to think before raising his hand. This was forgotten by the beginning of the next lesson when he would repeat the same pattern of behaviour.

Questioning – What It Is and Why It Matters

There are many statistics shared about questioning – that teachers ask two questions every minute, up to 400 in a day, equating to 70,000 over the course of a year. Up to a third of all teaching time is devoted to questioning our pupils.[1] Clearly, questioning is an important part of the teaching process, and it is inextricably interwoven with the other pedagogical principles discussed in this book. It is generally thought that questioning can lead to more effective learning than explanation or modelling can alone. Questioning can serve to enhance explanation and modelling, check basic recall of facts as well as deepen and develop understanding. In addition, we need to make it clear that we encourage and value pupils asking questions of us. Questions that stimulate thought, discussion and debate will, hopefully, encourage pupils to ask more of their own questions in return.

Some young children constantly question the world around them ("Why is the sky blue?" "Why doesn't the moon fall down?"), while others enter Early Years without a clear understanding of what constitutes a question. Our Early Years colleague, Emma Reid, begins by teaching the children what makes a question. They base questions around a visit from a mother and baby and plan in advance what questions

---

1   See Steven Hastings, Questioning, *TES* (4 July 2003). Available at: https://www.tes.com/news/tes-archive/tes-publication/questioning.

they could pose. When asked to suggest a question, some children will respond with, "I have a rabbit." Emma takes time with the children to explore why this isn't a question and leads them towards generating their own questions. It is undeniably important for children to have this understanding considering how many questions we ask of them!

If we are asking so many questions a day, have we considered the types of questions we ask? There are procedural questions that evaluate whether pupils are prepared or have completed tasks, questions that review previous learning, questions that interest and motivate pupils to get involved and questions that develop critical thinking skills and enquiring attitudes. When asking a question, we expect pupils to first listen to it, check their understanding of it, form a response in their mind, to sometimes voice this response aloud in the form of a full sentence and finally to revise or expand on this response if probed deeper by the teacher. Bearing in mind the many different types of questions and the stages of response that pupils need to progress through, the statistic that typically we allow just one second before expecting a response is surprising.[2]

Scripting questions in advance can help you to clarify the answer you are looking for and to anticipate any errors or misconceptions before they arise. Take this example: some Year 1 children may recognise that metals which are attracted to magnets are cold and shiny, and proceed to make an erroneous connection that all cold and shiny materials (such as glass) must also be magnetic. Knowing this in advance can allow the teacher to script questions that will dispel this misunderstanding.

---

2 See Hastings, Questioning.

This question generator may help you to vary the questions that you script.[3] Use one word from all or some of the columns.

why	is	identify	happen
how	did	describe	change
when	can	explain	cause
where	would	analyse	result
what	will	compare	affect
who	might	evaluate	find
		justify	same
			different
			advantage
			disadvan-tage
			improve
			agree
			disagree
			strength
			weakness

What follows are several questioning strategies that we, and other colleagues, have found useful in the primary classroom to help create a vibrant culture that encourages all pupils to opt in and actively participate.

---

3   Based on Allison and Tharby, *Making Every Lesson Count*, p. 233.

1. Mix It Up

Which type of question should I be asking?

No one type of question is intrinsically better than any other – they serve different purposes at different times. Closed questions, with a single correct answer and often beginning with 'who', 'what', 'when' or 'where', play an important part in checking understanding and ascertaining whether pupils can recall facts:

♦ Which countries share a border with England?

♦ How many wives did Henry VIII divorce?

♦ What material are fossils made of?

Open questions provoke pupils' thinking skills and require them to make connections with previous learning. They encourage the children to reflect and engage in discussion, because many open questions will not have a single correct answer:

♦ Why is this chapter a turning point in the novel?

♦ How can we encourage more tourism in our town?

♦ What do you think it was like to live during the Stone Age?

We ask many questions during the course of a day. Closed questions lead to quick-fire answers that keep a lesson flowing, and it can become a habit to allow this type of questioning to predominate. Ted Wragg's thorough and detailed research in primary schools has revealed that typically only 8% of questions asked are of an open, higher order nature.[4] He observes that a variety of questioning techniques will elicit a wider and more advanced range of responses than a preponderance of short, factual recall questions.

---

4 Ted Wragg, Types of Questions [video] (4 November 2015). Available at: https://www.youtube.com/watch?v=ffP9ocNQ6SU.

We would recommend being aware of the type of questioning that takes place in your classroom and ensuring that, while not overlooking the importance of factual recall questions and checking pupils' understanding, you pose open questions that encourage children to reflect in order to deepen understanding, generate lively debate and, in turn, motivate pupils to ask their own questions.

2. The Three-Second Rule

How long should I pause after asking a question?

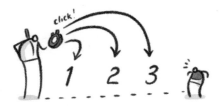

It is widely thought that most questions asked in the classroom are answered within one second of being posed – either by the first child responding correctly, the question being passed to another child or the teacher answering themselves. A sobering fact is that we tend to give less able children less time to answer – we make an assumption that they won't know the answer and quickly throw the question to another pupil as we don't want to cause them embarrassment. Think back to Amy at the start of this chapter – she's already anxious and we compound this by giving her less time to answer.

A simple strategy is to increase the length of time that we wait for an answer. Try to count out three seconds before accepting an answer – it will feel awkward at first but persevere. It is surprising how many more hands will be raised during those two extra seconds. Not only will the number of children willing to offer a response increase, but the quality of the answers should increase as well. Szymon, who we also met at the start of this chapter, will have more time to formulate an answer, so there is a greater likelihood of him answering thoughtfully. Following the three-second rule for factual recall questions allows the optimum wait time.

For questions that aim to encourage children to engage more deeply, try leaving more than ten seconds of thinking time. It takes time and practice to resist the urge to shorten the time, so rehearsing a sequence beforehand will help you to experience how long ten seconds feels. To help with this and to generate more detailed answers, Mel often narrates quietly during this time:

You have twenty seconds to think about the answer to this question ... Be prepared as I might call on any of you to answer... Remember to support your answer with evidence from the text ... Three, two, one ... Rosie, share your thoughts with us, please.

Try not to narrate over the entire thinking time as, ultimately, silence – real time to think – is crucial. After accepting a response, try waiting for a further second before offering feedback as this often serves to prompt the pupil to revise or expand on their response and it gives other pupils an opportunity to contribute.

Another tried-and-trusted method to encourage participation is to use talk partners, although you need to make sure that each partner is listening as well as sharing their own ideas. This can give pupils more confidence to volunteer an answer as they have a chance to rehearse an answer out loud. A variation when accepting responses is to ask the child to explain what their partner's ideas were; in this way, both partners are encouraged to take an active role in the discussion.

Another variation on this strategy is to give the children thinking time as part of a home learning task, with content often being delivered through an online video prior to the lesson. This enables the pupils to choose the time and pace that bests suits their needs, enabling them to revisit the content as many times as they wish to ensure that they come to the lesson prepared.

At the beginning of a series of Year 6 lessons on persuasive writing, the children were given links to several famous speeches – by Winston Churchill, Martin Luther King and a topical political party's election manifesto. The pupils were asked to listen to them several times, involve parents or older siblings in discussing them and come to the next lesson with a list of the features of persuasive speeches that they were able to identify. Amy, the pupil mentioned earlier, came into class with a piece of paper folded several times. She unfolded it and revealed a page of carefully written notes. She participated in the class discussion knowledgeably and was visibly more relaxed during the lesson. Szymon was also able to make valuable contributions to the discussions due to making use of thinking time prior to the lesson.

Here are some ways this strategy can be employed:

♦ MFL – to meet new vocabulary or grammatical concepts.

♦ English – to review prior learning, such as features of persuasive writing via video or auditory links.

♦ Maths – to introduce new concepts with the ability to rewind, review and think carefully about the content of a video.

♦ Science – to look at concept cartoons or videos and come to lessons prepared to discuss their views.

3. Involve Everyone

How can I ensure that I am engaging all pupils with my questioning?

We all aim to ask questions that generate a response from every pupil, even if not all responses are spoken out loud. However, we are often drawn to call on the same reliable individuals, especially when we are keen to round up a discussion and move on. The same six to eight individuals who are directly in our line of vision are more likely to be asked to respond. Dylan Wiliam notes that research has shown that "high-engagement classroom environments appear to have a significant impact on student achievement".[5] If pupils who actively participate and engage with questioning are more likely to make good progress, how do we encourage more pupils to participate? A combination of approaches is likely to prove most successful.

Hands up

In recent years, the typical classroom scenario whereby a question is asked and children volunteer answers has been out of vogue – the argument being that this induces a small

---

5   Wiliam, *Embedded Formative Assessment*, p. 81.

group of keen or extrovert children to dominate, while others do not engage with the question, fairly certain that another child will answer. The teacher might then make judgements about how well the pupils have understood the concept based on interpreting the responses of these few individuals. We would argue that there is a place for asking pupils to raise their hands as part of a much wider strategy to involve everyone – a simple show of hands in response to a factual, closed question can provide a wealth of formative information at a glance. You can, of course, combine asking some children who have raised their hands with asking others who have kept their hands down to respond.

An approach favoured by Allison and Tharby encourages teachers to direct questions to specific individuals.[6] Pupils should be aware that you are not looking for hands to be raised and that they should all have an answer ready. This sends a clear message that you expect all pupils to opt in. An advantage of this technique is that the teacher is less tempted to ask those keen, outgoing pupils and can instead target questions at less confident pupils, giving them the opportunity to participate and build their self-confidence. The teacher can also check the understanding of specific pupils and draw them in.

These directed questions should be embedded into your routine and be seen by the pupils as a positive chance to demonstrate their knowledge. Posing the question, pausing and then directing the question to an individual child will help to keep all pupils focused on having an answer ready. Consider the difference:

Teacher: Matthew, how can you work out the area of the triangle?

Teacher: How can you work out the area of the triangle ... Matthew?

---

6   Allison and Tharby, *Making Every Lesson Count*, p. 223.

Every pupil responds

As an alternative to hands up, Dylan Wiliam refers to "all-student response systems".[7] These could involve positioning thumbs up, horizontal or down to indicate levels of confidence, or fist to five by showing a clenched fist or the appropriate number of fingers. He cautions that the type of question asked should invoke a response based on thought rather than feeling (as self-reports can be unreliable) – for example, an incorrectly punctuated sentence could be written on the board and the pupils invited to come up to correct it. The teacher could then ask the pupils to indicate with a simple thumbs up/thumbs down whether the sentence is now correct and gather data by quickly scanning the responses. In the same way, the use of mini whiteboards is an effective way to involve everyone in contributing an answer. It is important to establish a clear routine, such as '3,2,1 ... show me', so that every child shows their board at the same time, rather than having time to alter their answer after seeing someone else's response.

Random responders

Random responders to questions can be selected in several different ways: low-tech lolly sticks or 'hands down' online name generators to name but two. All the children need to be prepared as there is no option to opt out. An advantage for the teacher is that they are far less likely to subconsciously exclude any members of the class or only direct easier questions to those children who may struggle. Consider putting the lolly sticks back into the pot when a pupil's name has been called so they aren't tempted to relax and sit back after their 'turn'. Taking random responses can add a different element to your questioning, but bear in mind that there are other strategies described in this chapter that

---

7 Wiliam, *Embedded Formative Assessment*, p. 88.

provide more valuable information for us as teachers and send a more subtle message to the pupils.

4. Serve, Return and Raise the Challenge

How do I ensure that pupils not only opt in but also give detailed and thoughtful responses to my questions?

The simplest way to avoid asking isolated questions is to make sure that there is always a follow-up question. As mentioned previously, it is important to stay with a pupil and support them to reach an answer to a question if they are unsure. However, it is equally important to stay with a child who answers our questions with ease – we need to probe more thoroughly and encourage them to deepen their understanding by answering a more complex question or justifying their answer. Knowing our pupils well helps us to keep them in the struggle zone, with the appropriate level of challenge.

An effective way of doing this is to follow up with a question beginning with 'Why?'

Teacher: How has the author highlighted that the two men are not bringing good news ... Ahmed?

Ahmed: They are wearing dark clothes and not smiling.

Teacher: Why does that make them stand out?

Ahmed: They stand out because it is a bonfire party and everyone is having fun.

Teacher: Why do you think the author has portrayed them in this way?

Ahmed: I think she has portrayed them this way because she wants to contrast their clothes and unsmiling faces with the laughter at the party. It warns the reader that they are not bringing good news.

Pupils may need to be supported to answer challenging questions by posing a series of questions that scaffold their thought processes. Art teacher Helen Cooper does this when encouraging pupils to analyse a painting. This is how Helen introduces *Tiger in a Tropical Storm* by Henri Rousseau. Rather than asking them to comment on what they can see in the painting – which often leads to a superficial discussion of the colours used – she guides their thinking, moving from closed to open questioning:

Can you see the grass swaying?

Is the sky darkening?

Are the trees bending over?

Why are there silver lines in the sky?

She then moves on to asking the children to explain how they know there is a storm ahead and that the tiger is frightened, eliciting that it is starting to rain and the tiger is crouching in the grass with eyes wide open.

When studying Van Gogh's *The Potato Eaters*, Helen encourages the pupils to look at the detail in the painting in order to understand what Van Gogh is portraying. She plans a series of questions by thinking about her end-point question – what season of the year is portrayed in the painting? By staging the questions in this way, she encourages all the pupils to follow the reasoning path so that the answer to each question builds on the previous one:

Teacher: Who is in the picture?

Pupil: There are five people, men and women.

Teacher: What can you tell me about their faces?

Pupil: They aren't smiling.

Teacher: What does the light do?

Pupil: It creates shadows on their faces and in the room.

Teacher: What time does it show on the clock?

Pupil: It shows 7 or 8 o'clock.

Teacher: Why is the lamp lit?

Pupil: It must be dark outside.

Teacher: Which season must it be?

Pupil: It must be winter as it would be lighter in summer.

---

5. All Opt In

How do I move past "I don't know"?

Take Amy in the opening scenario – anxious about being selected to answer a question and worried whether her peers will laugh at her if she gives an incorrect answer. To keep lessons pacy, it's so tempting to call on another child quickly, but what message is this sending to Amy? A culture where all opt in not only sends a message to each pupil that everyone is expected to be an active participant in the learning process, but also reminds us that, as teachers, we need to stay with the pupil and support her through the struggle to find an answer. Doug Lemov suggests that a child's anxiety can be alleviated by asking a simple question first. For example, Amy's teacher could ask: "Were you able to come up with an answer, Amy?"[8] Even if Amy responds with no, you can ask her to share how far she got with the question.

Here are some strategies to try:

♦ Rephrase the question to check for understanding. It is important to pitch a question in a way that the whole class understands in order to involve as many children as possible.

♦ Break the question into chunks:

Teacher: Which words are determiners in the phrase 'two apples on the table'?

Pupil: I don't know.

Teacher: Which words are nouns?

Pupil: Apple and table.

Teacher: A determiner gives us more information about a noun. Which words give us more information about 'apple' and 'table'?

Pupil: Two and the.

Teacher: Now, tell me which words are determiners in the phrase?

Pupil: Two and the are the determiners in the phrase.

---

8   Lemov, *Teach Like a Champion 2.0*, p. 255.

♦ Provide the pupil with options from which to select:

> *Teacher: How do you think Nat is feeling at this point?*
>
> *Pupil: I don't know.*
>
> *Teacher: At the top of page 59, it says that his hands gripped his rucksack tightly. Do you think he is feeling anxious or excited?*
>
> *Pupil: I think he is feeling anxious because he is gripping his bag tightly and also his eyes were darting about.*

♦ Give the pupil the answer and ask them to explain why it is correct:

> *Teacher: Can you identify the adverb in this sentence?*
>
> *Pupil: I don't know.*
>
> *Teacher: The adverb is 'gently'. Can you explain why this is the adverb?*
>
> *Pupil: It tells us how he placed the book on the shelf.*

♦ Ask another child, returning to the original child to repeat the answer:

> *Teacher: What is a prime number?*
>
> *Isaac: I don't know.*
>
> *Teacher: Katie, can you tell me what a prime number is?*
>
> *Katie: A prime number is only divisible by one and itself.*
>
> *Teacher: Isaac, your turn.*
>
> *Isaac: A prime number is only divisible by one and itself.*

6. Exchange and Build

How can I encourage pupils to listen and respond to each other?

Well-planned questions allow us to stretch the abilities of all the pupils in the class as we are able to make deliberate choices about the way we word questions, leading to more precise questions and, hopefully, more thoughtful answers. As well as listening and responding to us, though, it is important to cultivate a classroom environment where pupils listen and respond to each other. Szymon, in the second scenario at the start of this chapter, would benefit from developing these skills rather than being focused solely on the contribution that he would like to make to the discussion.

Share the questions

A simple strategy to encourage the pupils to focus on each other's answers is to create a 'why chain'. For every answer, create a new 'Why?' question to be answered by the next pupil:

Q: Why is 'to treat others as you wish to be treated' regarded as the Golden Rule?

A: Because most religions believe this.

Q: Why do most religions believe this?

A: Most religions believe this because respect is an important value.

Q: Why is respect an important value?

Bounce the questions

Another strategy to encourage pupils to listen to each other's responses is to pose a question to the first pupil (remembering the three-second rule) and then bounce the next question to another pupil:

Teacher: How can you change the atmosphere in your writing … Alice?

Alice: I could change the adjectives.

Teacher: What do you think of that … George?

George: I think verbs are more powerful at indicating a change in atmosphere.

ABC feedback

One way to build bouncing the questions into a discussion is to use ABC feedback – asking the pupils to Agree with, Build on or Challenge.[9] Once introduced and embedded with the class, the teacher asks the pupils if they would like to ABC:

---

9 This questioning approach comes from Alex Quigley's *The Confident Teacher: Developing Successful Habits of Mind, Body and Pedagogy* (Abingdon: Routledge, 2016).

Teacher: Would you like to ABC ... George?

George: I would like to build on Alice's comment by ...

Some children will take this to the next level: "I partly agree ... but also would like to challenge ..." Be insistent that the children use formal language and answer in full sentences.

7. Real-Time Response

How can I prepare in advance yet remain flexible in lessons?

While planning key questions or a series of increasingly challenging questions in advance can help to shape a lesson, we need to remain adaptable and ensure that we are listening carefully to the responses that pupils are giving us. Dylan Wiliam refers to this as listening "interpretively".[10] He makes the distinction between teachers who are listening for the correct answer, responding to answers with "Almost ... try again" – sometimes unwittingly sending a message to their pupils that they are in a hurry to get on with the rest of the 'script' – and those who are listening to the pupils' thinking and trying to work out how they could explain content better in future to help the pupils' understanding develop and avoid misconceptions arising. There will be times when you need to circle back and re-teach or clarify key points and other times when you will want to extend the challenge. Remember that we should aim to keep children in the struggle zone, so we need to listen to their responses to our questions with this in mind.

---

10 Wiliam, *Embedded Formative Assessment*, p. 85.

Take a cross-section

In Chapter 5, we refer to checking rather than marking books – a time-efficient way of finding out just how well pupils have understood a new concept or idea. Similarly, to assess comprehension at the end of a lesson, try listening interpretively by directing a series of questions to a cross-section of the class. Although not wholly reliable, it will give you a sense of the understanding of the class.

Reflective Questions

♦ What balance of questions am I planning to ask?

♦ Am I giving my pupils sufficient time to think before asking them to respond?

♦ Am I scripting questioning sequences that will give shape and direction to my lessons?

♦ How can I ensure that my questioning deepens pupils' understanding?

♦ Am I listening interpretively and building on my pupils' responses?

Final Thoughts

We used to think that confidence in life led to success in learning. In recent years, our reading of educational research, books and commentaries, alongside our experiences in class, has encouraged us to rethink this belief. We believe that children who are successful in their learning gain confidence through this success. Success cannot be defined by the government or a test and it certainly isn't about labelling children. It is unique and personal to each individual, and it is our job as teachers to help our pupils to experience it, in whatever way is appropriate to them.

One of the books we read was *Making Every Lesson Count* by Shaun Allison and Andy Tharby. We thought it was inspiring and were keen to take the six key pedagogical principles and write a version designed for primary teachers. We have drawn on evidence from cognitive science and well-respected educational thinkers and bloggers to inform our writing. In addition, it has been a pleasure to have talked to so many dedicated colleagues about their experiences in class, and we are indebted to them for sharing their ideas and strategies with us.

This has been an invaluable experience for us and we have learned so much from discussing and debating the strategies used in our school and their underpinning theories. Daily, the great teachers we work and interact with inspire us to think over, and rethink, what happens in our lessons. We aim for excellence in our teaching and we recognise and learn from the many mistakes we make.

We would encourage you, having read this book, to discuss the six principles with your colleagues; share your own suggestions and find out about new ideas to try. The strategies detailed in each chapter can be taken and experimented with in your classrooms. They have been developed over many years and across the primary age range. Feel free to adapt the ideas in this book for your classroom or school – we would be interested in hearing about your experiences. We truly believe that these strategies can have a positive impact on teaching and learning, and can help children to experience success in their learning and so to build confidence for their future.

One person who is deeply passionate about the future of children worldwide is Sheryl Sandberg, chief operating officer at Facebook. She introduces one video from her 'Lean In' series with the following: "Education is everything. When children get the high quality education they deserve, it opens up a lifetime of choice and opportunity."[1]

Throughout their primary years, children meet dedicated teachers striving to give them exactly this, laying each brick in a solid foundation for future teachers to build upon. Ultimately, it is up to each child to decide what they create with that foundation, so we hope this book gives you some ideas to ensure that every lesson along the way counts.

---

1   Quoted in Rahel Gebreyes, Sheryl Sandberg Teams Up with DonorsChoose to Support Schools in Need, *Huffington Post* (3 March 2016). Available at: http://www.huffingtonpost.com/entry/sheryl-sandberg-donors-choose-bestschoolday_us_56e1a619e4b0b25c918101a4.

Bibliography

Allison, Shaun and Andy Tharby (2015). *Making Every Lesson Count: Six Principles to Support Great Teaching and Learning* (Carmarthen: Crown House Publishing).

Bandura, Albert (1977). *Social Learning Theory* (Oxford: Prentice-Hall).

Berger, Ron (2012). Austin's Butterfly: Building Excellence in Student Work [video]. Available at: https://vimeo.com/38247060.

Berger, Ron (2003). *An Ethic of Excellence: Building a Culture of Craftsmanship with Students* (Portsmouth, NH: Heinemann).

Berger, Ron, Leah Rugen and Libby Woodfin (2014). *Leaders of Their Own Learning: Transforming Schools through Student-Engaged Assessment* (San Francisco, CA: Jossey-Bass).

Clarke, Shirley (2008). *Active Learning Through Formative Assessment* (London: Hodder Education).

Corbett, Pie (2004). *Jumpstart Literacy: Games and Activities for Ages 7–14* (Abingdon: Routledge).

Drews, Doreen and Alice Hansen (eds) (2007). *Using Resources to Support Mathematical Thinking: Primary and Early Years* (Exeter: Learning Matters).

Drury, Helen (2015). *Mastering Mathematics: Teaching to Transform Achievement* (Oxford: Oxford University Press).

Dunlosky, John, Katherine A. Rawson, Elizabeth J. Marsh, Mitchell J. Nathan and Daniel T. Willingham (2013). Improving Students' Learning with Effective Learning Techniques: Promising Directions from Cognitive and Educational Psychology, *Psychological Science in the Public Interest* 14(1): 4–58. Available at: http://www.indiana.edu/~pcl/rgoldsto/courses/dunloskyimprovinglearning.pdf.

Dweck, Carol S. (2006). *Mindset: How You Can Fulfil Your Potential* (London: Robinson).

Dweck, Carol S. (2007). The Perils and Promises of Praise, *Educational Leadership* 65(2): 34–39. Available at: http://maryschmidt.pbworks.com/f/Perils+of+Praise-Dweck.pdf.

Dweck, Carol S. (2015). Carol Dweck Revisits the 'Growth Mindset', *Education Week* (22 September). Available at: www.edweek.org/ew/articles/2015/09/23/carol-dweck-revisits-the-growth-mindset.html.

Elawar, Maria C. and Lyn Corno (1985). A Factorial Experiment on Teachers' Written Feedback on Student Homework, *Journal of Educational Psychology* 77(2): 162–173.

Elliott, Victoria, Jo-Anne Baird, Therese N. Hopfenbeck, Jenni Ingram, Ian Thompson, Natalie Usher, Mae Zantout, James Richardson and Robbie Coleman. (2016). *A Marked Improvement? A Review of the Evidence on Written Marking* (London: Education Endowment Foundation). Available at: https://educationendowmentfoundation.org.uk/public/files/Publications/EEF_Marking_Review_April_2016.pdf.

Ericsson, K. Anders, Ralf Th. Krampe and Clemens Tesch-Romer (1993). The Role of Deliberate Practice in the Acquisition of Expert Performance, *Psychological Review* 100(3): 363–406. Available at: http://www.nytimes.com/images/blogs/freakonomics/pdf/DeliberatePractice(PsychologicalReview).pdf.

Gebreyes, Rahel (2016). Sheryl Sandberg Teams Up with DonorsChoose to Support Schools in Need, *Huffington Post* (3 March). Available at: http://www.huffingtonpost.com/entry/sheryl-sandberg-donors-choose-bestschoolday_us_56e1a619e4b0b25c918101a4.

Gladwell, Malcolm (2008). *Outliers: The Story of Success* (London: Penguin).

Hastings, Steven (2003). Questioning, *TES* (4 July). Available at: https://www.tes.com/news/tes-archive/tes-publication/questioning.

Hattie, John (2014). Interview with Sarah Montague for *The Educators* (25 August). Available at: http://www.bbc.co.uk/programmes/b04dmxwl.

Heath, Chip and Dan Heath (2007). *Made to Stick: Why Some Ideas Take Hold and Others Come Unstuck* (London: Arrow Books).

Herrmann, Erick (2014). The Importance of Guided Practice in the Classroom, *MultiBriefs* (12 February). Available at: http://exclusive.multibriefs.com/content/the-importance-of-guided-practice-in-the-classroom/education.

Ikeda, Miyako (2011). School Autonomy and Accountability: Are They Related to Student Performance? *Pisa in Focus* 9 (Paris: OECD). Available at: http://www.oecd.org/pisa/pisaproducts/pisainfocus/48910490.pdf.

Kirby, Joe (2016). No Excuses: High Standards, High Support, *Pragmatic Education* (10 December). Available at: https://pragmaticreform.wordpress.com/2016/12/10/no-excuses-high-standards-high-support/.

Lemov, Doug (2015). *Teach Like a Champion 2.0: 62 Techniques That Put Students on the Path to College* (San Francisco, CA: Jossey-Bass).

McDaniel, Mark A., Ruthann C. Thomas, Pooja K. Agarwal, Kathleen B. McDermott and Henry L. Roediger (2013). Quizzing in Middle-School Science: Successful Transfer Performance on School Exams, *Applied Cognitive Psychology* 27: 360–372. Available at: http://www.academia.edu/2417836/Quizzing_in_Middle-School_Science_Successful_Transfer_Performance_on_Classroom_Exams.

Mei, Liu Yueh and Soo Vei Li (2014). *Mathematical Problem Solving – The Bar Model Method: A Professional Learning Workbook on the Key Problem Solving Strategy Used by Global Top Performer, Singapore* (Singapore: Scholastic Teaching Resources).

Oakhill, Jane, Kate Cain and Carsten Elbro (2014). *Understanding and Teaching Reading Comprehension: A Handbook* (Abingdon: Routledge).

Peat, Alan (2008). *Writing Exciting Sentences* (Biddulph: Creative Educational Press).

Plowden, Lady Bridget (chair) (1967). *Children and Their Primary Schools. Report of the Central Advisory Council for Education (England)* [Plowden Report] (London: HMSO).

Quigley, Alex (2016). *The Confident Teacher: Developing Successful Habits of Mind, Body and Pedagogy* (Abingdon: Routledge).

Reynolds, Peter H. (2004). *The Dot* (London: Walker Books).

Rogers, David (2016). Fall Down Seven, Rise Eight. Can Schools Grow Grit? *David Rogers* (27 May). Available at: http://www.davidrogers. blog/?p=31/.

Skemp, Richard (1976). Relational Understanding and Instrumental Understanding, *Mathematics Teaching* 77: 20–26. Available at: https://alearningplace.com.au/wp-content/uploads/2016/01/Skemp-paper1.pdf.

Smith, Jim (2017). *The Lazy Teacher's Handbook: How Your Students Learn More When You Teach Less* (Carmarthen: Independent Thinking Press).

Syed, Matthew (2015). Viewpoint: Should We All Be Looking for Marginal Gains? *BBC News* (15 September). Available at: http://www.bbc.co.uk/news/magazine-34247629.

Tidd, Michael (n.d.). Why More Tests Are a Good Thing, *Teach Primary*. Available at: http://www.teachprimary.com/learning_resources/view/why-more-tests-are-a-good-thing.

Tidd, Michael (2015). Why We've Got Planning and Marking All Wrong (Part 1), *Ramblings of a Teacher* (5 November). Available at: https://michaelt1979.wordpress.com/2015/11/05/why-weve-got-planning-and-marking-all-wrong-part-1/.

Wiliam, Dylan (2011). *Embedded Formative Assessment* (Bloomington, IN: Solution Tree Press).

Williams, Sir Peter (2008). *Independent Review of Mathematics Teaching in Early Years Settings and Primary Schools. Final Report* [Williams Review] (Nottingham: Department for Children, Schools and Families).

Wragg, Ted (2015). Types of Questions [video] (4 November). Available at: https://www.youtube.com/watch?v=ffP9ocNQ6SU.

Making Every Science Lesson Count

Six principles to support great science teaching

Shaun Allison

ISBN: 978-178583182-9

Writing in the practical, engaging style of the award-winning *Making Every Lesson Count*, Shaun Allison returns with an offering of gimmick-free advice that combines the time-honoured wisdom of excellent science teachers with the most useful evidence from cognitive science.

Making Every Science Lesson Count is underpinned by six pedagogical principles – challenge, explanation, modelling, practice, feedback and questioning – and provides simple, realistic classroom strategies that will help teachers make abstract ideas more concrete and practical demonstrations more meaningful.

In an age of educational quick fixes, GCSE reform and ever-moving goalposts, this precise and timely book returns to the fundamental question that all science teachers must ask: 'What can I do to help my students become the scientists of the future?'

Suitable for science teachers of students aged 11–16 years.

Making Every English Lesson Count
Six principles to support great reading and writing
Andy Tharby
ISBN: 978-178583179-9

Writing in the practical, engaging style of the award-winning *Making Every Lesson Count,* Andy Tharby returns with an offering of gimmick-free advice that combines the time-honoured wisdom of excellent English teachers with the most useful evidence from cognitive science.

Making Every English Lesson Count is underpinned by six pedagogical principles – challenge, explanation, modelling, practice, feedback and questioning – and provides simple, realistic classroom strategies to bring the teaching of conceptual knowledge, vocabulary and challenging literature to the foreground.

In an age of educational quick fixes, GCSE reform and ever-moving goalposts, this precise and timely book provides practical solutions to perennial problems and inspires a rich, challenging and evidence-informed approach to English teaching.

Suitable for English teachers of students aged 11–16 years.

Making Every Lesson Count

Six principles to support great teaching and learning

Shaun Allison and Andy Tharby

ISBN: 978-184590973-4

Making
every lesson
count

*Six principles to support great
teaching and learning*

Shaun Allison and Andy Tharby
Foreword by Doug Lemov

Packed with practical strategies and case studies, *Making Every Lesson Count* bridges the gap between research findings and classroom practice. The authors examine the evidence behind what makes great teaching, and how to implement this in the classroom to make a difference to learning. Using case studies from a number of schools, the authors demonstrate how an ethos of excellence and growth can be built through high-quality classroom practice. Combining robust evidence from a range of fields with the practical wisdom of experienced, effective classroom teachers, the book is a must-read for trainee teachers, experienced teachers wishing to enhance their practice and school leaders looking for an evidence-based alternative to restrictive Ofsted-driven definitions of great teaching.

A toolkit of strategies that teachers can use every lesson to make that lesson count. No gimmicky teaching – just high-impact and focused teaching that results in great learning, every lesson, every day.

ERA Educational Book Award winner 2016. Judges' comments: "A highly practical and interesting resource with loads of information and uses to support and inspire teachers of all levels of experience. An essential staffroom book."